FREE DAYS WITH GEORGE

Free Days with George

with George

Learning Life's Little Lessons from One Very Big Dog

Colin Campbell

DOUBLEDAY CANADA

Doubleday Canada and colophon are registered trademarks of
Random House of Canada Limited.

LIBRARY AND ARCHIVES CANADA CATALOGUING IN PUBLICATION

Campbell, Colin, 1962-, author
Free days with George : learning life's little lessons from
one very big dog / Colin Campbell.

Issued in print and electronic formats.
ISBN 978-0-385-68287-9 (bound). ISBN 978-0-385-68288-6 (epub)

1. Campbell, Colin, 1962-. 2. George (Newfoundland dog).
3. Human-animal relationships. 4. Marketing executives--United States--
Biography. 5. Marketing executives--Canada--Biography. 6. Surfers--
California--Los Angeles--Biography. I. Title.

SF422.82.C36A3 2015 636.70092 C2014-907479-4
 C2014-907480-8

Unless otherwise stated, all photos are courtesy of the author.

Printed and bound in the USA
Cover and book design by Jennifer Lum
Cover images: (George) courtesy of the author; (tag) © Pixelrobot | Dreamstime.com;
(tag ring) © Elisabeth Burrell | Dreamstime.com
Image on page 1 and 207: © Olgacov | Dreamstime.com

Published in Canada by Doubleday Canada,
A division of Random House of Canada Limited,
A Penguin Random House Company

www.penguinrandomhouse.ca

10 9 8 7 6 5 4 3 2 1

Penguin
Random House
DOUBLEDAY CANADA

In memory of my grandfather Nick Howes, who taught me to embrace and love the ocean, the value of a strong work ethic, and to recognize and cherish free days.

HERE ARE A FEW THINGS I KNOW:

I know that the people who matter most to me in my life are those who can look me in the eye.

I know that I love the ocean and that it brings me back to myself.

I know that my grandfather, the man who taught me how to swim and how to live life to the fullest, remains one of my most important mentors and guides, even though he died many years ago.

And I know that one of the most powerful experiences of my life so far has involved my deep and abiding friendship with a dog named George, who brings all the things I know together.

Prologue

I am a swimmer and a surfer. I love the ocean. My dog, George, a 140-pound Landseer Newfoundland, also loves the water. I hesitate at the language here, because "my dog" makes me sound like I own this being I share much of my life with. As I hope you'll see in this book, George is possessed only by himself, and we humans lucky enough to know him and to have had our lives touched by him are merely the recipients of his generous gifts.

George is the dog who changed my life. When I was at my worst, he was there to comfort me. He was homeless when I took him in as a "rescue," but as it turns out, he's the one who rescued me. He taught me how to walk and how to wait, how to sit and be patient, and how to accept and embrace change. He taught me the power of hugs, to whisper instead of yell, to listen more deeply to others around me and to be sensitive to those in need. He taught me to ride the waves of life instead of letting them wash over me and drown me. He taught me you can swim out to sea too far—and he's towed me back to the safety of shore more times than I can remember. He taught me that the sport of surfing, like life, can't be taken too seriously—that sometimes just getting up on a board is all you need to do to make yourself and those around you happy.

Many of the life lessons I learned with George were reminders of lessons I'd learned long ago. Isn't it true that often without our recognizing it, life comes full circle?

My grandfather Nick Howes was the first positive force in my life, and in so many ways he was my first teacher. He began teaching me the lessons that George would later bring home to me when my grandfather no longer could.

So let me rewind a bit here and tell you about my grandfather Seymour Wylde Howes III. He was born on a sugar plantation on the Caribbean island of Montserrat in 1913. He preferred to be called "Nick." I called him "Grandpa." A decorated World War II hero, he was one of the first to arrive on the beaches of Normandy, France, on D-day, where he saved several of his fellow soldiers from drowning after their landing craft struck a mine. After the war Grandpa lived what would be deemed by most standards a modest, ordinary life. Yet to me, he was anything but ordinary.

My younger brother, David, and I had a very close relationship with our grandfather. Grandpa lived his life passionately and selflessly, making us feel special in both little and big ways that would help shape our lives for years to follow. As boys, we used to spend all summer at his cottage on a serene beach in a quiet cove in Nova Scotia, Canada. Most mornings we woke up to the smell of sizzling bacon and the sound of my grandfather's deep, enthusiastic voice. "Get up, lazy bums!" Grandpa would bellow as we lay in bed. "Today is an important day! We have important things to do!" According to my grandfather, we had "important things" to do every day.

"Let's see . . ." he'd say, standing in the doorway to our room. He'd be checking an invisible schedule that hovered outside beyond the cottage's picture window, somewhere down where the ocean lapped the shores of the sandy beach. "We have swimming to do today. And

5

sand castle building. Then we have lawn mowing, and firewood chop-
ping, and more swimming. Then we have sailing, followed by a quick
trip into town for some grocery shopping. Then we have a barbecue
scheduled. Then I'm pretty sure we have some blueberry-pie eating to
get in there right after. Then we are going to finish with some tooth-
brushing, pajama wearing and bedtime-story reading."

My brother and I would listen to this from the warm comfort of
our bunk beds, pretending to be asleep, until Grandpa would say, "But
before we get to all that, I've got to get you lazy bums out of bed!" And
with that he would launch at us and tickle us through a mound of
blankets as we laughed and giggled and laughed some more.

No matter how old we got—for years, for a decade—that's how
we started every summer day with him.

He ended our days almost the same way. After our agenda of
chores and fun, dusk would be upon us before we even realized it. We'd
be dog tired as we changed into our pjs and prepared for bed. He would
come in to read us a story, and before he would turn out the light, he
would ask, "Boys, did you have a good day?"

"Of course we did, Grandpa!"

"You know, boys," he'd say, his voice soft and gentle, "today was a
free day."

"What's a 'free day,' Grandpa?" we would ask without fail.

With a big smile he would look down at us and say, "A free day is
when you spend a whole day doing things you love to do—like building
sand castles, flying kites or going swimming. And when you do those
things with people you love who love you, you don't grow old that day.
It's a free day." He would pause and brush the hair off our faces as he
looked deep into our eyes. "Today, boys, we had a free day on earth.
Today we didn't grow old. Sleep tight. I love you."

Then Grandpa would switch off the light, and we'd drift off into

a rich, deep sleep. We loved him with our whole hearts, and he loved us back even more.

It was only much later in life, after I lost what I loved the most and long after Grandpa was gone, that I learned how hard "free days" are to come by in this life. I forgot what they felt like until George helped me find them again. Now, with George's help, I try to make every day a free day.

Under Water

ONE

The clouds had covered New York City all day, a rumpled gray blanket thrown over the skyscrapers. It was February 2008, and cold enough that even if New York refused to sleep, New Yorkers would certainly have preferred to stay bundled up in bed. Those unlucky enough to have dragged themselves upright and out into the cold world now hurried through the streets with miserable determination, their collars turned up and their coats pulled tight against the chill. I was in New York on a business trip, and all I could think of was finishing my day of meetings and flying home to my lovely wife of four years. None of the chill and chaos bothered me, because soon I'd be flying home. Soon I'd be with Jane.

I was working as an executive for MKTG, a hip marketing firm based in New York City. I loved working there—these were the smartest, most innovative people who I had ever worked with. They were professional and fun. I ran their Canadian office in Toronto. I had come to New York to follow up on a television show we had pitched to NBC. A couple of weeks prior, we had convinced NBC's vice president of sports programming to green-light a sports reality

show I had created. Life was great. I had a beautiful, loving wife and a great job working with smart, nice people.

That morning I had found myself awake and looking out the window across the rooftops an hour and a half before my alarm was set to go off. I couldn't sleep anymore, so I texted Jane to see if she was also awake. Moments later, instead of the *ding* of a return message my phone rang.

"Hey, you're awake!" I said.

"Kind of," she answered, laughing, her voice still soft with sleep. "I saw your text."

"I'll let you go back to sleep," I said, just above a whisper. "But it was nice to hear your voice. Thanks for calling."

"When's your first meeting?"

"Nine thirty."

"You'll do great." I could hear her smiling.

"Thanks, it should go okay."

"I love you. Good luck. Call me later."

"I will. I love you, too," I said.

I hung up happy to have heard her voice. Even though my job allowed me to travel all over the world, stay in great hotels and eat in fantastic restaurants, I always missed Jane when I was away. Our work schedules often took us away from each other, but that time apart made me appreciate more the moments I got to spend at home. To me home meant Jane.

I got up, showered, dressed and headed to my first meeting, which went better than I'd hoped. My colleagues and I decided to go out for an early lunch before diving into our afternoon meetings. I was scheduled to fly out that night, but by the time we finished eating, the wind had kicked up and turned the sky into a deep bruise of dark purples and gray. Snow hadn't started to fall yet, but the news services were

broadcasting a winter storm warning and I knew the odds of my plane taking off as planned were diminishing fast. As I watched New Yorkers scramble to get back to the warmth and the shelter of home, I felt a powerful urge to do the same. I didn't want to be stranded in an airport. I wanted to go home. I wanted to see my wife. I wanted to be with Jane.

Jane and I met almost fifteen years earlier at a fund-raising dinner in support of the United Way. She was someone who always stood out from a crowd. She was prettier, taller, blonder and more vibrant than anyone else in the room. I'd seen her from a distance, speaking to another attendee, and I was awestruck by her natural poise and elegance, not to mention her smile. It made me melt. When I got within a few feet of my assigned table, I realized that not only was she seated at my table but my chair was right beside hers. My heartbeat pounded in my ears, drowning out every noise in the room.

Before I could get too nervous, a hand extended toward me. "Hi, I'm Jane."

We talked about the weather, the Toronto Blue Jays, our jobs—mundane things—but in her presence they took on a new significance. She was a reporter covering the fund-raiser for a local newspaper. She immersed herself in our conversation and made me feel I was the most fascinating person in the room. I could see she was razor sharp and worldly. She also swore like a sailor—not too many women can pull that off. And I loved it. Halfway through the entrée, I already had the feeling we had a connection and I'd met someone special.

At the end of the evening, I suggested we stay in touch, and we exchanged business cards. As I was leaving, I told a colleague I was going to marry that girl. He laughed. "She can probably marry

whoever she wants to, and it likely won't be you." I laughed back and said, "You wait."

I picked up Jane's business card repeatedly over the next few days. To call or not? I wanted to wait a sensible amount of time and not seem too eager. I lasted all of a day and a half before inviting her out for coffee. I left her a voice mail at work, and while I waited for an answer, I told anyone who would listen that I'd met this incredible woman. I acknowledged I was getting a bit ahead of myself—I really didn't even know her yet—but at that moment, I didn't really care.

Jane called me back a day later. We went for coffee. After some enthusiastic small talk she told me she had just started to see someone. She said she couldn't deny the spark between us at the fund-raiser, but she was serious about this other guy. She wanted to be up-front about her relationship, she said, because she still wanted to be friends. I was disappointed, but I wanted to be part of her life any way I could. Also, call it youthful arrogance, but I seriously thought it was only a matter of time before she dumped that other guy and chose me. After all, she was the woman I was going to marry. We were going to spend the rest of our lives together. It would just take her a little longer to realize it.

Over the next few months, we settled into a warm friendship. As difficult as it was not to flirt with her, I did my best to respect her boundaries. But I still made any excuse to see her. Through work, I signed up for Meals on Wheels, a volunteer program to deliver meals to disadvantaged people in the community who aren't always able to cook for themselves. When I found out you needed a partner to make the deliveries, I phoned Jane and asked if she'd be mine.

"Definitely," she said. "When do we start?"

"This Wednesday at noon. Or next week—whatever's better for you."

"I could do this week. It's a date."

"Awesome," I said, grinning my head off. "I'll pick you up from work." Delivering meals meant that for ninety minutes every week I'd get to see Jane. I knew the volunteer work wouldn't be glamorous, but knowing that Jane would be there was all the glamour I needed.

From our first delivery, the division of labor was clear: Jane knocked on the doors and did most of the talking to the clients; I carried in the big bag of food. Our clients lived in subsidized housing in one of Toronto's roughest, most impoverished and violent neighbor-hoods. These were people life had beaten down. Some were older, and many had been all but abandoned by their families. Others were living with HIV/AIDS, and over the weeks and months, we watched them waste away before our eyes, even as we delivered them nutritious food. Both Jane and I could feel their loneliness and desperation, and we did our best to offer some kindness and quiet support. Friends would ask me how I handled this without getting depressed. "It's easy," I'd answer. "I do it with Jane."

Crossing the threshold of each opened door, Jane brought with her the same rapt attention she'd bestowed on me the night we met—always making a profound impact. I watched, spellbound, as person after person fell in love with her. And I couldn't help but fall deeper and deeper in love with her myself. The more time I spent with her, the better I got to know her. And the more I knew her, the more I felt that my initial impulse to spend the rest of my life with her was not so crazy after all.

Every week she would turn her attention to me before we got started. She'd look me right in the eye and ask, "How are you, Colin? What's new with you? What's good in your life?" It's a common thread in my life: the people who have the most meaning to me look me right in the eye—my grandfather, my good friend and boss Charlie, Jane. And later, my dog, George. Whenever Jane looked at me like that, I felt connected and answered her questions eagerly. She

in turn would tell me amusing stories about her work or her friends, and we would laugh together and commiserate. Spending time with her was comforting and familiar, and in that weekly meeting we managed to make a cold, depressing, hidden part of the city our haven. At the end of the delivery we would shake hands and she'd say, "Have a good week." I'd wave and smile as I walked away. Then I would miss her for the next seven days.

This went on for months, becoming a predictable rhythm in my life. Occasionally our paths would cross at other work-related events. Seeing her was always great and my feelings of wanting to marry her never faded; in fact, they only got stronger. Then one day Jane called me out of the blue, and it had nothing to do with our volunteer schedule. "I'm wondering if we could grab a coffee," she said. She sounded different, more serious than usual.

"Of course," I said.

A few days later we met at a Starbucks. She seemed nervous and fidgety, but when she sat down across from me, she eyed me with that direct, almost intimidating gaze of hers. Calmly she said, "I think I know how you feel about me and I know there's something special between us. I really value what we have as friends and so I wanted you to hear this from me before someone else says something."

I sensed that whatever was coming next wouldn't be good.

"I'm getting married."

For more than two years I'd dealt with not being able to be with her by pushing my feelings aside. But in the background, I'd never shaken the belief that she would eventually break up with this guy and choose me. When she shared this news, I was crushed and knew I couldn't see her anymore, even as a friend. I made the best of it in the moment—I smiled and told her I was happy for her and wished her luck. But from that point on, I made a conscious effort not to see

her. She didn't need me in her life. Reluctantly it was time for me to move on.

By 2004, which was many years later, Jane was no longer on my mind. I was still single, had quit my job in Toronto and moved back to Nova Scotia to be near my grandfather. He was in poor health and I wanted to make the most of the time he had left. He was an anchor to me when I was growing up, and I wanted to return the love and care he'd given me as a boy. My grandfather was the most passionate person I've ever met, a man who lived life to the fullest no matter what he was doing—fixing a car, telling a joke, hosting a barbecue or swimming with his grandsons at the cottage.

Helping take care of my grandfather meant being away from my normal life for quite a long time. I still made semi-regular trips to Toronto for business and to visit friends, and it was on one of those trips—to see my accountant in the early days of March—that I ran into Jane. She was at a crosswalk in the financial district, waiting for the light to change. She was partially hidden under a big winter jacket and hat, but it was her, all right. While over the years I had tried to move on—thought I had—the moment I saw her I knew I had not done a very good job.

I watched her get closer and closer after the light changed. Then I caught her beautiful pale-blue eyes brighten as she noticed me. Her face broke into a beaming smile and she reached out and gave me a huge hug. I held her in the middle of the intersection, too stunned to speak. A taxi trying to turn the corner started honking at us, so I put my arm around her and ushered us over to the safety of the sidewalk.

"I heard you'd moved away," she said, out of breath. "I heard you were in Halifax."

All I could get out was "Yup."

"What are you doing back in Toronto?"

I told her that I was in town for just a day and that I had moved out east because my grandfather was not doing so well.

"I'm really sorry to hear that," she said. "I remember every time you talked about him it always put a giant smile on your face."

"Thanks. I just want to spend some time with him while I still can."

Then she asked, "Would you like to have dinner tonight?"

I was due to fly out in a couple of hours, so I did the only thing I could in order to see her: I lied. "I don't leave until tomorrow. Sure—I'd love to have dinner!"

I changed my flight and met her downtown in the bar of the King Edward Hotel. We ate and drank and caught up on each other's lives. She told me that she had separated from her husband.

"He wasn't the guy I thought he was," she said, lowering her gaze and studying her hands in her lap. "We just drifted. It didn't work out," she added. "I've actually thought about you a lot recently."

And that's when she paused, looked me right in the eye and stated, "I married the wrong man."

I couldn't believe what I was hearing. In the years since I'd met her, I'd dated other women and had even had a few meaningful relationships. But I'd never felt what I had with Jane, and I'd never been able to fully give myself to anyone else. Now, here Jane was, sitting across the table from me and saying the thing I'd always hoped she'd say. I felt elation, vindication, excitement. A little confusion. A ton of shock. And love. I thought my face would split in two from smiling. I told her I felt as strongly about her as I always had, that I loved her and had always loved her.

"So, do you think we can make up for all the time we've lost?" she asked.

"Yes," I said. "Yes, we can."

A year later, on a beautiful fall day in front of forty of our closest family and friends in a tiny church right on the ocean in Boutiliers Point, Nova Scotia, enveloped in the comforting scent of maple wood burning in the woodstove, we were married.

It was the happiest day of my life.

I remembered all this on that frigid afternoon in New York City four years after I had married Jane, as the storm threatened to ground all planes at LaGuardia Airport. It still hadn't yet started to snow, so there was still a chance I'd make it out of the city if I hurried. I took a break from silently willing the taxi through traffic to call Jane. "They haven't canceled any flights yet but they will soon, so I'll try for the earliest available."

"So I'm still going to see you tonight?" she asked, trepidation in her voice.

"I hope so."

"What time do you think you'll get back?"

"Around dinnertime if I can get re-routed."

"Please try," she said.

"You know I will."

At long last I arrived at the airport, to find everyone there in full-fledged revolt. Businessmen with compact suitcases viciously elbowed their way through groups of panicked tourists, and airport workers were being grilled like key witnesses in a murder trial. The line snaking from the Air Canada desk was impossibly long and full of screaming children. I took my place at the end. After what seemed like hours, I was finally face to face with an Air Canada employee having one of the worst days of her life.

"Hanging in there?" I asked as I placed my ticket on the counter.

"Just barely," she said. "People go crazy in bad weather. How can I help you?"

I took a deep breath. "I know this is probably the same thing everyone's asking," I began, "but I'm looking to get home to Toronto as soon as I can. I don't think my flight's going to make it out tonight, and if you could help me find an alternate route, I'd really appreciate it."

She took my ticket and asked for my passport. Then she began typing away at her computer. A few moments later, she glanced up and flashed me a smile. "All the current Toronto-bound flights are full. I may be able to get you on a flight to Charleston. It's not affected by the snow. From there we have a direct flight to Toronto, and you should make it home just fine."

"That would be perfect," I said. "And thank you."

She printed out my new boarding pass and handed it over the counter.

I called Jane when I deplaned in Charleston. "I'm stuck here for about two hours, but I made it out of New York."

"I thought you'd be home around dinnertime." She sounded disappointed, maybe even a bit annoyed.

"This is the best I could do. If I hadn't come this way, I would've been stuck in New York for I don't know how long."

"I guess," she said. This time she definitely sounded annoyed.

"I'm sorry. I wish I were already there. But I'll be home soon. That's the important thing. I love you."

There was a short pause, and then she said, "See you soon."

TWO

I made it home to Toronto just before midnight on what turned out to be the coldest night of the year. Snow lay thick on either side of the runway, but the dark sky was clear and dotted with stars. As the plane taxied up to the gate, I pulled out my phone and sent Jane a quick text: "Back safe. It's late. Don't worry about picking me up. I'll grab a taxi." I was exhausted, but I didn't want her to have to leave the house so late, especially considering it *felt* like the coldest night of the year. I couldn't help but smile when her reply came a minute later: "Don't worry. Already on my way." It's amazing how good something little like that can make you feel.

Standing on the curb, I dropped my bag on the asphalt and turned my back to the wind. I tried to warm myself up by thinking about the vacation Jane and I had been talking about. I pictured us lying on a beach in Barbados, our favorite vacation destination, the sound of the surf licking at the shore, lounge chairs pushed right up against each other as we read under the sun, always making sure that some body part was in contact—fingers just touching, legs in a lazy tangle. I held the vision for a minute and then opened my eyes to snow-covered cars driving by, splashing salt-infused slush up onto the sidewalk. As I breathed, the hair in my nostrils froze.

Jane's Ford Escape rounded into view. One last leg—a short, warm car ride with the person I loved most in the world—and I could drop my bag, ditch my coat and curl up in bed with her. When she pulled to a stop in front of me, I was grinning like an idiot.

I opened the rear door and threw my bag in the back. Then I jumped into the passenger seat, shivering a little. "Man, am I glad to see you." I leaned in for a kiss across the console.

"Welcome home," she said, before pecking me on the mouth. Then she turned back to the steering wheel and pulled away from the curb. "How are you? How was the flight?" She was wearing her puffy parka and a knit tuque, from which a few stray strands of her golden hair had fallen loose. She looked cozy and adorable. I was so happy to see her.

"So, how were your meetings?"

"They went great. We're really starting to get things together for the show—it's pretty exciting."

"That's awesome!" she said, taking her eyes off the road for a moment and flashing a smile.

I filled her in on a few more details and asked how her days had been.

"Oh, it was all fine," she said, shrugging off the question. "Are you hungry at all? We don't have much to eat at the house, but I can stop somewhere."

"I'm okay. I just want to get home."

For me at that moment in my life "home" had extra meaning. Never had any other house I'd lived in felt so much like a home. And that was mostly because I associated the place with Jane; all our memories as a married couple were stored there. Its location—across from a park, looking out at a children's playground on a quiet one-way street in the east end of the city—was what we'd fallen in love with first. The house itself had good bones. We got it at a decent price

because its last major repairs had been done in the 1960s. Over three and a half months, with friends and family pitching in here and there, we gutted then totally rebuilt the place. We installed new wiring and plumbing—using three-quarter-inch pipe instead of half-inch, so the water pressure was amazing—redid all the drywall, turned three tiny bedrooms into two bigger ones with vaulted ceilings, renovated the kitchen, repaired the roof and the front porch and tore off the old aluminum siding to reveal a red-brick exterior. We even hired "brick hippies" to clean and restore the beautiful old brick. Though we'd lived together for more than a year already when we bought it, it meant something extra that we'd renovated the house together rather than piggybacking on someone else's work.

Jane had a way with plants and put it to use in the perennial beds we laid in the front yard. My thumb was less than green, but I still loved working out there alongside her. At the end of a long summer day's weeding and watering, we'd sit on the porch with a couple of glasses of wine and admire our handiwork as the sun set over the park.

The night Jane drove me home from the airport it struck me as odd that she pulled up in front of the house. A laneway led to the garage at the back of our property, but she didn't turn into it. "Hey," I said, "you missed the laneway."

She didn't respond at first, just steered smoothly and brought the car to a stop alongside the curb. She put the car in park but didn't kill the engine. Keeping both hands on the wheel, she waited a beat, and then, looking straight ahead, she announced, "I'm not going in."

Kind of a rough joke to lay on me after the travel ordeal I'd just been through. "Okay, sure," I said, chuckling. "Seriously, though, why are we out front?"

The beat was longer the second time, but the answer was the same: "I'm not going in, Colin."

This time I registered her tone. It was a cold, clipped monotone, robotic and completely unrecognizable. The smile disappeared from my face. "What do you mean?"

"I mean I'm not going in," she said yet again. She continued to stare straight ahead, her expression fixed and unreadable. In the fifteen years I'd known her, it was the first time I could remember her not looking me in the eye as we spoke. "Colin, I'm very unhappy and I've been unhappy for a long time. I need some time to think and I need to do it away from here. I'm going to stay at a friend's house."

Suddenly I couldn't breathe. I felt like I was underwater. Panic struck me right in the gut. I remembered when I was in university and spent my summers lifeguarding at a park in Nova Scotia called Rissers Beach. To get the job, I took advanced CPR and first aid, and passed a host of extreme fitness and swimming tests. Throughout the training we were taught again and again that in emergency situations the biggest killer is panic. If you panic, you waste energy—you can't focus on keeping your head above water and swimming out of danger. If you yell for help and swallow water, you panic even more, and eventually you go under. The importance of keeping a level head was drilled into us, and having that ability was prized above any amount of strength or endurance. Sitting in that car, with the heat vents blasting and my pulse racing so fast and loud I felt like my heart was trying to push its way out the side of my chest, I couldn't think rationally. For the first time in my life I felt pure, unfiltered panic—like I was drowning.

"What? What are you saying? And where are you staying?" I asked. "Who are you staying with? Why are you doing this? What do you need to think about?" The questions came out as fast as I thought them. She said nothing.

"Jane, this is crazy," I said. "Look, we are smart, logical people. I love you. We can figure this out."

"I told you already." Her face was a mask, her voice filled with aggravation. "We're different people. Like I said, I've not been happy for some time, and I've decided to leave. This isn't about you and it's not about us. This is my decision and I've already made it."

I felt sick and cold and I'd broken out in a sweat. "Just come inside," I pleaded. "Let's just go inside. We can talk about this."

"I—am—leaving, Colin." She enunciated each word as though speaking to someone who didn't understand English. "There is nothing you can say. You need to let me go. Please get out of the car."

I knew then that my only hope lay in getting her out of the car and into the house so I could make sense of what was happening, so I could just talk to her until the old Jane was back and this whole nightmare went away. But my mouth wouldn't move. I sat silently, defeated, tears running down my cheeks. She didn't turn her head or look at me, yet she seemed to soften slightly. "It's only for a few days," she said. "I just need to think for a few days. I'll call you."

In my state of panic I snatched at this hope. If it's only for a few days, I thought, then fine. I'll go in the house and regroup, and she can go figure herself out and she'll come to her senses. She will come home. I reached into the backseat for my bag and got out of the car. She drove away the instant I closed the door.

The front door was no more than twenty feet from where Jane had left me. I felt like I was walking in a daze, while at the same time barely holding in a scream. The snow crunching under my boots was the only sound. Even though it was eighteen below, my face felt like it was burning. I have no idea how long it took me to reach the porch. When I made it to the door, I reached for my keys but dropped them. I bent to

pick them up and I noticed how violently my hand was shaking. I drew a breath and tried the lock, but whether from the cold or the shock, I couldn't steady my hand enough to open the door. I tried again, then a third, fourth and fifth time. After several minutes the lock finally clicked and the door swung into our home—Jane's and mine.

I put my suitcase down in the front hall. I can't remember closing the door. I turned on the entrance light, and when I went to the hall closet, I noticed that all Jane's coats, scarves, sweaters, hats and shoes were missing. I ran up the stairs to our bedroom with my coat and boots still on. I dropped to my knees in front of our dresser and started pulling out drawers. All Jane's clothes were gone. Half the bedroom closet was empty, too. I stood and walked to the upstairs bathroom. My breath came difficult and shallow. Shampoos, conditioners, moisturizers, creams, lotions—not just a few days' worth of supplies—all gone. Stumbling back downstairs, I passed half-empty bookshelves and pale patches of wall where pictures had hung. She'd scrubbed any trace of herself from our home. All that was left in her place was empty space.

In the kitchen I threw open every cupboard. Most of our plates, mugs and glasses—things we'd bought together—were still there, but our good plates, the ones we used when company came over and the ones that Jane had owned before we met, were gone. Faint circles in the dust on the credenza marked where they'd sat.

Afraid of what else I might find missing, I opened the door to our unfinished basement and descended the wooden steps into the dark. It was colder down here. My chest felt more constricted, like I was suffocating. The only light was a bare bulb with a pull chain. I reached up and tugged it. A workbench ran along one wall, with all my tools neatly arranged. The area at the far end of it where Jane stored her gardening equipment was empty. Her bike was gone, too. The rush of tears nearly choked me. It was February 25, one of the coldest days

of the year. Spring was still months away . . . and she'd taken her bike? And that was when it hit me: she's not coming back.

My legs gave out from under me and I fell to the floor. I cried harder than I thought I could for longer than I thought I could. I struggled for breath but didn't try to get up. At some point I stopped crying and lay still under the light of the bare bulb. I listened to the furnace switching on and off. I stayed there for hours. It was the longest and the worst night of my life.

THREE

What do you do with yourself when the love of your life has left you?

The light in the room must have changed gradually, the slice of sky visible through the basement windows shifting from dark blue to the faint pink of sunrise. But I didn't notice it had gotten bright out until the sun climbed high enough to shine directly onto my small patch of floor. I hadn't slept. I was stiff from spending the whole night curled in a ball on a concrete floor. But the physical pain suited my mood. Something compelled me to try to act as normal as possible—almost as if I were on autopilot. I decided to go to work. I hauled myself up the basement stairs, showered, and changed my clothes, doing my best not to look around the house as I moved through it. I went outside and got in my car and drove the fifteen minutes to work. I was so distracted I probably could've run down half a dozen people on the way without registering the thuds.

The Toronto office of MKTG was in a nondescript low-rise office building off Yonge Street. I shuffled to my desk feeling numb and dangerously over-stimulated at the same time. Not many of my co-workers were around and it was a quiet day. I felt completely detached, as though I

were outside of my body, watching myself move through the day. Of course I tried calling Jane, at her office and on her cell, only to get an automated answering machine voice. I tried over and over, to no avail.

Around three in the afternoon I decided to stop and get some lunch. I had no appetite, but I hadn't eaten since the airport in Charleston. I also needed to get some air, even if it was still frigid out. I shrugged into my jacket, pulled on my hat and gloves and headed for a deli a couple of blocks from the office.

I could feel the leaden weight of my legs, and the freezing air burning my lungs and tearing at the exposed skin of my face, but I couldn't shake the sensation that I was floating somewhere above and ahead of my body. I observed myself bent into the wind, trudging up the street, the pain and humiliation written on me so clearly I might as well have been wearing a sandwich board with My Wife Just Left Me stenciled on it. Everyone I passed could tell. How could they not? A voice close by me cut through the wind. "Hey, buddy, I had a rough night. Spare some change?"

He wore a bulky, stained overcoat over layers of loose clothing all turned roughly the same brownish gray by dirt, time and human grease. His face, hidden under at least a week's growth of beard, put him in his mid fifties, though he could've been younger and just worn by life. He had flattened himself a seat in a snowbank at the edge of the sidewalk, with a blanket under him to protect his legs against the cold. He wore big, clunky winter boots, beside which lay a pair of garbage bags that seemed to contain the rest of his worldly possessions. His eyes were trained on my face and lit with something I couldn't identify.

"Sorry?" I said.

"Spare some change?" he repeated.

"Yeah," I said. I found my wallet in my jacket pocket and freed a five-dollar bill. "Here."

His eyebrows gave away his surprise. He took the money and looked me over again. "Hey, thanks," he said. "Rich guys don't usually give me anything."

I was far from rich; and it was uncharacteristic of me to stop and talk to homeless people, plus I never gave them money. But in that moment there was something about him I could relate to. Though he wore his struggles more visibly than I wore mine, we'd both had a rough night.

He reached into his coat and pulled out a bottle wrapped in a brown paper bag. "Want a drink?" he asked, moving the bottle a few inches toward me.

Normally I wouldn't even think of accepting a drink from some homeless guy, and I'm not a big drinker at the best of times, but his offer actually seemed to make sense in that moment. "Yeah, sure, what the hell," I said, taking the bottle from him. Whatever was in it tasted like lighter fluid. I let it burn the back of my throat and felt it light up my empty stomach. I handed the bottle back. "Thanks."

He took a drink of his own and then slid his hand back into his coat, to conjure a pack of cigarettes from an inner pocket. "Wanna smoke?" He held out the pack and gestured at it with his chin.

I didn't smoke, either, but that didn't stop me from pulling a cigarette from the pack. "Thanks," I said as he handed me his lighter and tried to stand, then stumbled and tipped back into the snowbank, instead. I slipped a hand under his arm and helped him to his feet, then lit the cigarette he'd given me and held out the flame for him to light his. I handed him back the lighter and took a long drag on the cigarette. The smoke felt good in my lungs, calming, like it was the first full breath I'd drawn that day. I didn't cough. I exhaled a cloud into the air. "How'd you end up on the street?" I asked.

His answer was long and confusing. It involved a farmhouse and a beautiful wife who'd dumped him; friends who'd betrayed him; his

grade-five teacher and the government, both determined to strip him of everything he owned. After staring at my computer screen all day, I found this a welcome conversation. When my cigarette was done, I thanked him and told him to look after himself. "Yeah, buddy," he said. "Come back tomorrow. I'll be here." I walked off toward the deli and never saw him again.

The rest of that first day and the two that followed it are lost in a haze that would become familiar to me over the coming days and weeks. That first week I called and texted Jane dozens of times, asking her to meet with me or at least to pick up the phone and explain why she'd left and where she'd gone. No answer. I spent hours obsessing over every detail of our relationship, looking for clues that might explain her departure. I worked as much as I could, thirteen- and fourteen-hour days that often ended well after nine. At home I sat on the couch and tried to drown out my thoughts with beer and television. It didn't matter what was on—reruns, reality shows, infomercials—I just let the TV play until I could quiet my mind enough to fall asleep. I avoided the bedroom Jane and I had shared and slept on the couch, instead. I stopped cooking and cleaning and let the empty pizza boxes, soup cans, half-eaten frozen dinners and bottles pile up on the kitchen counter.

A few friends reached out early, not because they knew what had happened but because both Jane and I had fallen off the face of the earth. I didn't return their calls or emails. Jane and I had always been seen by our friends as "the ideal couple"—successful, deeply in love— and I was embarrassed to now acknowledge that maybe not everything had been as perfect as it had seemed. And how could I admit that I had

no idea why? But at the same time I somehow knew that I needed to take solace in other people. I just wasn't quite ready yet.

The loneliness reached a degree of intensity that made it truly unbearable. I had to tell someone, so I picked up the phone and called my younger brother, David.

Dave and I had grown up very close. We did everything together as kids. I started playing organized hockey at the age of five, and two years later he followed me into it. From then on hockey was the cornerstone of our relationship. We collected and traded hockey cards and pooled our money to pitch in on hockey magazines. We read everything we could about the Toronto Maple Leafs and Montreal Canadiens, and spent countless hours watching their games on TV. When we weren't absorbing the sport, we were out playing it. Every winter we played standard hockey in organized leagues, but also in forms we invented (as only kids can) when we couldn't get on the ice. The two of us played hockey on our knees in the family living room using our hands and a Ping-Pong ball or Popsicle sticks and an old pencil eraser. We scuffed up the basement playing with a tennis ball and full-sized hockey sticks. In the winter we ruined countless garden hoses trying to flood our backyard to make a rink, and in the summer we played in the street.

Because Dave was younger, I'd always felt protective of him. When our dad got mad or was being unreasonable, I did my best to shield Dave from him. No matter what happened, good or bad, we were always in it together. But that didn't mean we'd chosen the same path. He married straight out of university and settled down in the same Nova Scotia town where we'd both done our undergrad degrees. He became a teacher and then a school administrator, and he and his wife had two beautiful kids. His life was a model of stability and here I was calling him with mine in shambles. I'd failed in my marriage and that

made me feel I'd failed as his older brother. I was no longer the person he could lean on. When he picked up the phone, I could barely get out the words. But somehow through the tears I managed to tell him that Jane had left.

"You shouldn't be alone," Dave told me when I'd finished. "I'm on my way."

Visiting me meant leaving his wife and children, taking time off work and flying all the way from the east coast to Toronto. He'd made the decision in a matter of seconds. It was the nicest thing anyone had ever done for me. All I could say was "Thank you. I'm glad you're coming."

One day later Dave was in my living room. He could stay only for a few days, but his support—his mere presence—made it possible for me to get through that first week. Dave did whatever he could to keep my spirits up and my mind off Jane. He sat with me, helped me clean up the house a bit, took me to see a Will Ferrell movie that he knew would make me laugh. There was no elaborate technique to his methods of distraction, and only a few deeper conversations about what I was experiencing, but his very presence helped. I shudder to think how bad things might've gotten if he hadn't gone through so much trouble to show me someone in the world still loved me.

The day Dave left I fell back into a haze of depression, and the next day I finally heard from Jane: "I really don't want to see you," her text read. "I need more time to think."

I texted her back immediately: "This is crazy. We need to talk. Talking is going to help as much as thinking. We can talk and think together. Please come back to the house and we can have dinner tomorrow."

Her response: "I'm not ever coming back to the house. Ever."

"Not at the house then. But we do need to talk."

"I've thought about it and I want to be alone," she answered.

I should have been crushed, but after more than a week of total silence communication of any kind felt like a step in the right direction. After a few more texts we finally agreed to meet for lunch at a restaurant a couple of days later.

The night of that exchange of emails I went out and bought a pack of cigarettes for the first time in my life. I'd always been very anti-smoking and used to lecture my smoker friends about quitting. I took the pack and a few beers to the enclosed porch at the back of the house, sat in the dark and chain-smoked. Snow was falling softly. The porch was clean and quiet. It was peaceful at first. But after a while memories intruded. I found myself thinking of my grandfather. The first time I introduced Jane to him he was an old man living in a federal veterans' home. He looked her up and down, smiled softly and said, "I hope you will marry this boy." She beamed at him. He passed away just two months after Jane and I got married—our wedding was the last time he went out in public. Suddenly I felt his absence keenly.

There were many times growing up that I'd felt disconnected from my father. As a result my grandfather had often provided support and encouragement when I needed it most. As a World War II veteran he was a man who lived his life with the intensity and joy of someone who'd almost lost it. He was never short on advice, and as I'd been lucky enough to have him in my life into my forties, he'd helped me through most major decisions or problems I had faced.

I thought about what my grandfather would've done in my situation—the advice he would have given me. And that's when I started hearing his voice, as though he had joined me right there on the porch and was lighting up his pipe.

You don't see people smoking pipes anymore, but men of his generation loved them. As a kid, the smell of sweet cherry tobacco was one of my favorite things. In my mind's eye, he told me as he took

a puff of his pipe, "You shouldn't smoke. Don't do it just because I do. Your mother would not be pleased."

"Okay, Grandpa," I answered.

"You know, I started smoking during the war. Not saying it's right, but it helped calm my nerves when the bombs were going off and things looked really bad."

Things were looking really bad for me right now, and I actually felt okay smoking knowing that he used to.

Grandpa continued. "If you have a problem, the first step in dealing with it is to ask yourself, 'How did it start?'" He always said that when I came to him looking for help.

"Okay, Grandpa. How did it start?" When I finished my smoke, his voice dissolved.

I'd already spent hours searching my memories for clues about why Jane had left, yet the process had yielded almost nothing. Out on the porch I decided that despite all the love I had for her and how happy and proud I was to be her husband, maybe *I* was the problem. Maybe some flaw deep within me had caused her to go. If I could fix it, I reasoned, I might get her back.

The restaurant we'd agreed to meet at was downtown, part of an upscale strip cutting through an otherwise pretty run-down area of the city. The place was maybe half full, the diners a sea of business suits. She'd chosen a table for four in the middle of the room and was facing the entrance, with her coat and bag piled on the chair beside her. Her hair was pinned up from her face and she was wearing jeans and a dark sweater I'd always thought made her look too stern. She spotted me and fanned her fingers in the barest hint of a wave.

It felt strange not to hug her. The greeting we did manage was awkward and strained. A waitress came by and asked me if I wanted anything to drink, which gave me a little bit of time to recover my wits. When she left to get my water, I asked the first of the many questions that had been driving me insane. "Where did you go?"

"I found a place," she answered. "I'm going to live there for now."

I waited for her to continue. She didn't. The waitress returned, and walked into a thick silence. "Here's your water," she said, setting it in front of me on the table. "Can I get you two anything to eat?"

Jane ordered. I hadn't looked at the menu and didn't have much of an appetite, so I asked for the same thing she was having. The waitress took the menus and left. Another thick silence descended.

"So, you're not going to tell me where you're living now?"

"No."

"Why not?"

"I don't want to. It's none of your business."

"Jane, you're my *wife*. Of course it's my business."

Without consciously noticing, I'd raised my voice slightly. No one around us seemed to have taken much notice of me, but Jane stiffened as though she'd been slapped. "No, it's not actually your business," she said, one notch above a whisper. "And we're *not* going to have this conversation here."

This wasn't going well.

"Why are you doing this?" I asked.

"I just can't deal with marriage right now."

I didn't try to keep the hurt from my voice. "Do you mean, 'deal with *me*'?"

Maybe feeling that she'd gone too far, she looked at me with a measure of sympathy. She drew a breath. "I want to be on my own," she began. "It has nothing to do with you. I'm just more comfortable alone."

"This is crazy. Our marriage isn't disposable. My emotions aren't disposable—and I feel you're treating me like I am."

"I'm sorry. I don't want to hurt you," she said. "But I don't want to be married. We're different people and we need to just move on with our lives and find how to be happy that way."

As she was talking, the waitress brought our food. She put the plates down, offered the obligatory fresh-ground black pepper and asked if we wanted anything else. When she left, I made my big play.

"We need to go to marriage counseling," I said.

"Colin, it really won't change my—"

"Hear me out," I said. "I'm not just going to walk out the door without making an effort. I want us to go try counseling. If I have to change or fix something, I will. If we go and, after three months or four months or however long it takes, a professional marriage counselor looks us in the eye and says, 'There's no hope of rehabilitating this,' then I'll be the first one to shake your hand and wish you well. If we don't at least try to fix this, we're crazy."

I'd planned the speech and rehearsed it in my head a million times, but when it came to saying it, I got out maybe half of what I'd intended. Jane's face was completely unreadable, a mask. "I'll think about it" was all she said. She then made an excuse about having to get back to the office and bolted without saying another word. She'd eaten everything on her plate. I hadn't taken one bite, so I had my food packed up. As I walked out of the restaurant, I noticed a homeless guy on the street corner. I gave him my lunch and some money in exchange for a smoke. I stayed and talked with him for a while. Despite the misery of living on the street, he seemed happier than I was. I had to get out of there.

It took Jane another week or so to agree to counseling. I found a couples' therapist online and booked an appointment. Jane tried to back out two or three times in the lead up but turned up on time for the first session. Our counselor's office was full of plants and had two overstuffed, comfortable armchairs. The counselor seemed way too happy given the circumstances. Pictures of her family—united, happy, beaming—hung everywhere. It felt like she was showing off. I was having a hard enough time going to counseling in the first place. Her happy, smiling family wasn't making it any easier.

During the sessions that followed I had ample time to ask the many, many questions I had. Why had Jane left? Was I a terrible person? Had I done something wrong? Was I boring? Did I leave my socks lying around? Had she met someone else? Jane answered question after question by shrugging. When pressed, she'd give one- or two-word answers. Most of the time, she merely stared out the window, avoiding eye contact. The counselor took notes and tried to get Jane to talk. In our last session she said, "Jane, you do owe him a bit of an answer. Is there anything you can share about why you left?"

Her answer: "I just don't want to be married anymore."

At the end of each session Jane would bolt for the door. At the close of our last session, once Jane had left, the counselor asked me to stay awhile longer.

"Look," she said. "This isn't about you."

"What do you mean?" I asked.

"Jane obviously has some things she has to deal with on her own. They may not have anything to do with your marriage, but they seem to affect her ability to be in this marriage right now. We're not making any progress, so I suggest both of you seek individual counseling and deal with your own issues separately."

At this point I still believed that Jane would eventually come

around, but hearing the counselor's advice brought the truth home to me. My relationship with Jane was over.

"I guess you're right" was all I could say to the counselor. I left her office and for the first time started to give up hope.

When I wasn't at work, time went by in a blur. I was able to stay focused at the office, and invested all my energy into my job, which, thankfully, was still going quite well. I stayed at the office late into the evening most days, before coming home, eating whatever took the least effort to prepare and spending the rest of the night alternating between smoking on the back porch and sitting in front of the television. One particularly bad night, I was on the couch in the early hours of the morning when a mental health public service announcement came on the TV. In it, an unshaven actor wearing sloppy clothes was lying on a couch looking borderline catatonic. Whoa, that's me, I thought. Maybe I should do something about this.

My father always said that only crazy people go to therapists. In fact, before considering marriage counseling, those words were ringing in my head. His influence caused me to fear therapy and see it as a sign of failure and a source of ridicule. At a certain point, though, I just got sick of being miserable. Spring had arrived. The outside world became more inviting and I felt more and more like rejoining it. I slowly started to reconnect with friends. My old friend Catherine and her husband, John, had been among the first of my friends to reach out to me, and they'd taken me under their wing, inviting me to Sunday dinner and checking in on me frequently.

Catherine was a successful psychotherapist with a private practice in downtown Toronto. "You should talk to someone," she said.

"You mean, like, a therapist?" I asked.

"Yes. I can recommend a few people."

"Am I really that messed up?"

She smiled. "I think it would be helpful for you to have someone to talk to," she said.

With Catherine's help, my family doctor referred me to a psychiatrist. Dr. Edward Hamer's office was on the third floor of an old, eight-story, brown-brick medical building on Bloor Street. The entrance was wedged between a family-owned convenience store and a Shoppers Drug Mart. The directory in the lobby listed practitioners of every medical specialty known to humankind: dentistry, podiatry, otolaryngology, orthodontics, urology—and psychiatry, the specialty of the man who was supposed to guide me back to happiness. What the hell was I doing?

There was only one working elevator up to Dr. Hamer's floor. The size of a closet, it shuddered ominously as it climbed, and smelled of medicine and body odor. Dr. Hamer's office was at the end of a dingy hallway. I pressed the buzzer and a short while later I heard the *click* of the door unlocking. I tentatively opened it and found myself in an empty waiting room.

The room was poorly lit and smelled like mothballs. I sat down and picked up a well-worn *New Yorker* magazine and started leafing through it anxiously. I can't believe I'm doing this, I thought. I considered leaving, but just as I was readying myself to do so, the dark wooden door of Dr. Hamer's office opened.

A patient, who had obviously been crying, mumbled a quick thank-you and exited. Dr. Hamer was standing in the threshold of his office. He was a conservative and expressionless man with big glasses and thinning hair. He looked exactly the way I imagined a psychiatrist would. "Colin," he said, nodding at me in greeting. I got up and followed him into his office.

He spoke over his shoulder as he made his way to a green armchair near the head of a long leather couch. "As I mentioned on the phone when you made the appointment, before I agree to treat you, we need to run through an initial assessment. So today I'm just going to ask you a series of questions to get a sense of our best course of action and the type of help I may be able to provide." He stopped in front of the chair and motioned at the couch. "If that's agreeable to you, please lie down and we'll begin."

Lie down? Like, on a couch? "The assessment sounds okay," I said, taking a seat on the edge of the couch. "I'm fine to just sit like this and talk to you."

His expression remained neutral, but something in his voice changed. "If you don't lie down, I can't help you," he said.

"What do you mean?" I asked. "We can't have a face-to-face conversation?"

He shook his head slowly. "That's not how this works," he said. "If you want my help, you'll have to do as I ask and lie down."

I sighed and rolled my eyes . . . and then did as he'd requested.

I had expected him to ask me why I'd come, ask about Jane and my marriage and everything that had made me sad and broken enough to need psychotherapy. But when his questions began—then continued one after another—there didn't seem to be any clear theme or connection to my current crisis.

"Do you like your mother?" he inquired. "Do you like your father? Are you okay with heights? Confined spaces? Do you have any phobias at all? Are you an organized person? Are you punctual? Do you get along with others easily?"

I didn't tell the truth. Instead I gave Dr. Hamer the answers I thought he wanted to hear—the ones I thought were right. Sitting up on the couch to make eye contact with him pretty regularly, I painted an idyllic childhood, a family free from dysfunction. I made myself out

to be a perfectly stable, well-adjusted person with no irrational fears and anxieties. He didn't comment on any of my answers, just made notes on a large pad of paper that rested in his lap. Lying on my back like Charlie Brown at a therapy session with Lucy, I felt every bit as self-conscious and ridiculous as I'd expected. Dr. Hamer just kept firing away: "Do you see people who aren't really there? Do you hear voices in your head?"

"Well," I answered, "not loud ones." I was hoping for a laugh, but all I got was the sound of his pen scratching. "I was just joking."

Silence.

He started writing again.

"You don't have to write *that* down," I said.

He kept writing. "You're going to write down everything, aren't you?" I queried. He wrote that down, too.

The questions continued for more than half an hour. At the end of the session Dr. Hamer rendered his verdict: "You can come once a week, tell me how you feel and share your problems," he said. "It could help your immediate feelings. However, it won't be a long-term fix for you." He paused to let that settle in. "If you *really* want to get to the root of your issues, I recommend that you come four times a week."

Four times a week! Was I *that* crazy? Dr. Hamer continued before I could say anything. "I want you to know that the frequency isn't a commentary on you or the severity of your depression. Only certain patients can benefit from this kind of approach. Based on today's assessment, I think you're a candidate."

I was devastated; I must really be in trouble if I needed to see him that often.

"I don't know if I can handle four times a week," I told him. "At the very least, I'll have to see what I can do with my work schedule."

"You're free to think about it and get a second opinion," he answered. "But I'll need to know what you want to do within a few days."

"Okay, thanks," I said. "I'll consider it."

I got in touch with Catherine, who enthusiastically and passionately recommended moving forward with the therapy, calling it a real opportunity for emotional growth and telling me I'd feel much better if I did it. So, not feeling that I had a better option, I rejigged my work schedule, and started to see Dr. Hamer at the recommended frequency. It took some getting used to. Some days I'd spout like I'd had a few too many cups of coffee. Other days it would be too difficult to share my emotions, and I would walk into Dr. Hamer's office and, before I'd even made the couch, tell him, "I'm not talking to you today." We'd sit in silence for forty-five minutes and when the time was up, I'd leave. Whichever version of me showed up, Dr. Hamer would sit as expressive as a Buckingham Palace guard and methodically question and record every thought, impulse and life experience.

On one occasion, as I came into the room I mentioned it was a nice day out—just making small talk. "Really?" he asked. "Why is it nice?"

"The sun's out. It's warm . . . I was just being polite."

"What makes you think you need to be polite?"

"I don't know!" Everything with him, even the most innocuous small talk, turned into an inquisition. One time I got so frustrated with his incessant questioning I muttered "Idiot" under my breath.

"I heard you say that," he said. "Why do you think I'm an idiot?" And it began all over again.

It took three or four months, deep into the summer, but eventually I started to notice small progress in myself. Rather than helping me focus on Jane, Dr. Hamer had gone back to some of my earliest memories: the formative experiences behind quirks, fears and issues I often didn't even know I had. Some sessions would end with me shattered and crying, afraid to go back out into normal life, but occasionally, on breakthrough days, I started to make sense of things that had escaped

me my entire life. I still had trouble sleeping. I still missed Jane. I still over-worked and smoked and left the house a pigsty. But something in me was moving, changing.

I was getting better.

FOUR

I was almost back on my feet by the end of the summer, but I was also, in Dr. Hamer's words, "still pretty wobbly." Though I had managed to pull myself from my emotional rock bottom, I still hadn't managed to put all that much distance between Jane and me yet. There was a sense that any progress I'd made could unravel with one good pull, and as the summer slipped into fall—bringing back the cold and darkness that had been such bitter constants in the months when I was at my worst—I started to feel the first tugs on an invisible thread pulling me back down. I began to feel more and more anxious about being alone.

One suggestion for alleviating that anxiety came from a conversation with my friend Matt. Matt worked for a digital company that shared office space with MKTG. I liked Matt. He had recently graduated from university, worked hard, had a passion for hockey and had a dry sense of humor that always made me laugh—something I certainly hadn't been doing enough of. One day he dropped by my office and asked if I wanted to grab some lunch. Matt didn't know all the background about Jane and me, so I caught him up over our meal.

"That's a bummer," he said, before pausing to swallow his food. "But that might not be the worst thing in the world."

"Well, of course it's not the 'worst thing in the world,'" I said a bit sarcastically.

"Sorry. All I meant was that it's probably better not to rush into a relationship where someone's going to be expecting things from you. You've got to give yourself some time."

He was right. In fact, he was an echo. During my smoking binges out on the back porch, my grandfather continued to visit me, and one of the things he kept saying, in my head, was "Wait a bit, wait a bit. There's no need to rush things." Over and over again in that quiet, calm voice he used with me when I was a kid.

"I think it's just been bugging me because I feel a bit lonely in the house by myself," I now told Matt. "I've never felt lonely before. It's weird. The house is a lot of space for one person."

"You know what you should do?" Matt said, waiting a beat for effect. "You should get a dog." He was grinning as though he'd just solved global hunger.

"That's it, eh? That's the big solution?"

"That's it," he answered with total sincerity. He took a huge bite of his sandwich. "Think about it. Dogs are loyal—they aren't going to pack their stuff up and leave for no reason. As kids we always had dogs. My family helped train guide dogs for the blind. They're great! You'll get out and walk around a lot, meet people . . . maybe meet a hot girl. It'll be amazing. It will change your life."

"It will change my life," I said, imitating him.

"It will. And you have a big, empty house right across from a park."

We finished eating and walked back to work without any more dog talk, but over the next few weeks, once a day or so when we passed in the office, he'd ask me, "So, you get that dog yet?"

"Still thinking about it."

A few hours later he'd poke his head into my office. "So, you know who man's best friend is?"

"Not Matt," I'd reply.

It went on and on like this, day after day. I pretended I wasn't listening, but in truth I gave the idea of getting a dog some thought.

By mid December, I got an email from Matt. Its subject line: "Get that dog yet?"

The email went something like this:

Hey Colin,

No pressure, but I thought I'd send you this link for a great dog website, Petfinder.com. It's like a dating site, but instead of pretty girls who will probably see your picture and never write you back (ha-ha), this one is full of dogs that don't care what you look like but want your house and the park across the street. Beats a cage any day.

Take a look. You can give a dog a good home and get some company in return. And I might stop nagging you. And you would be saving a life.

Let me know if you need any help.
Matt

Matt wasn't too far off on his dating-site comparison. Petfinder aggregates information about rescue animals available for adoption all over North America. Each dog gets its own profile page with information about its breed and background. There were thousands of lonely dogs looking for their "forever homes." But as I scrolled down the pages, one of the pictures stopped me in my tracks.

This dog was a Landseer Newfoundland, unlike any dog I'd seen before. Striking, with the typically Newfoundland pitch-black head perched atop a vast white body. There was nothing in the picture to measure him against, but something about the way he held himself, head up and chest out, gave an aura of immensity. He had a long, shaggy coat, floppy ears and a soft muzzle with a dusting of white above his nose, but what leaped out at me most were his eyes. They were a dark brown that seemed light against the black sea of his face. Sparkling with intelligence, they also looked weighed down by experience, with lower lids that drooped to expose a pair of pink half-moons. They were the eyes of an old soul. He was just over a year old and they listed his name as Kong.

Then reality set in. What in the world was I doing? The last thing I needed in my state was to adopt a dog that no doubt had his own problems. Did I not have enough problems myself? Who did I think I was that I wanted to save the world, when I couldn't even get myself on an even keel? Yet, looking into those eyes, I was compelled to do something. How could anyone abandon such an incredibly beautiful dog? Could I really handle a dog this big? But before I knew what I was doing, my fingers were on the keyboard, tapping out a response to Matt:

Matt,

Thank you for hounding me (pun intended). This is a great site. I saw one dog in particular that's making me seriously think about your advice.

I'll let you know how it goes.
Colin

Over the next few days I did some research into the Newfoundland breed. Despite being among the largest dogs, with some males tipping the

scales at over two hundred pounds, Newfoundlands are considered the gentlest of all breeds and are revered for their nurturing and gentle nature with children. (Nana, the nursemaid dog in *Peter Pan*, was a Newfoundland.) Newfs have webbed paws and are expert swimmers. They were specifically bred in Atlantic Canada to haul nets and to save fishermen from drowning by towing them to safety. They are noted for their bravery and loyalty, with many of them having served for Allied troops in both world wars.

I thought back to my grandfather and his service during World War II, when his troop carrier struck a mine and sank 150 yards from shore and my grandfather took it upon himself to rescue his injured comrades. He wrapped their arms around his neck and, one by one, towed them to shore. He was decorated for his bravery.

When I was done researching Newfoundland dogs, I researched shelter dogs a bit more and learned that in 2012, in the United States alone, over 2.7 million abandoned dogs were put to death. That's 6,267 a day. I also learned that younger, smaller dogs tend to get adopted sooner; older dogs and big dogs are not so lucky. Finally, I learned what a big, red URGENT banner means when it appears beside a dog's profile. It means that animal is nearing its expiry date. At overcrowded municipal shelters a dog is usually kept for only seventy-two hours, after which, if it isn't claimed or adopted, it will be euthanized. Then the dog's profile is quietly removed from the website.

I looked at Kong's picture over and over. He had been abandoned. I felt I had to do something, for him as much as for myself. That Newfoundlands are bred as ocean rescue dogs certainly sealed my interest. I love the water. Always have. My happiest memories of being a kid were at my grandfather's cottage in Nova Scotia, where we spent hours swimming in the ocean each summer. There were days when the only time my brother and I came out of the water was when we were called out to eat. In university I worked as a lifeguard and taught myself how to surf.

My friend Mike and I were among the first people in Nova Scotia to pick up the sport, which has since grown popular there. I also worked with the Canadian Coast Guard, doing inshore search and rescue as a summer student. Getting a dog that loved the water appealed to me. I imagined the dog and me walking along the shore of Lake Ontario. I imagined the joy of having a companion, of not having to walk alone. A few days after Matt first sent me the link, I called the contact number.

The woman who answered was a volunteer with a Newfoundland rescue organization called Newf Friends, which keeps tabs on local shelters and maintains a network of foster homes for Newfoundland dogs in need. When a Newfoundland turns up in a regular shelter, Newf Friends places the animal with a suitable foster home until a permanent home can be found. The organization's extremely dedicated staff of volunteers ensures that even amid the upheaval that comes with life in foster care, abandoned Newfs are cared for by people with a genuine passion for and understanding of the breed. Their efforts to care for Newfs outside the shelter system have saved the lives of many of these gentle giants.

"So which dog are you calling about?" the volunteer asked me after some small talk.

I told her about Kong and his Petfinder post.

"Oh yes. He's a lovely dog. He came from a home in a small town about a two hours' drive north of Toronto. He is a bit skittish, but he's making progress."

"Skittish?" I said.

"There were some issues. However, we like to focus on addressing a dog's current behavior and potential rather than talking a lot about the past. What's important is that this dog is adapting well to the current, more favorable environment. That really is good news, you know."

Obviously there was a lot more, which she wasn't going to tell me right away, so I let it be. I learned that Kong was being fostered by a

family who owned a farm. The woman assured me that he couldn't be in more capable hands. She took down my address and said she'd send me some forms to fill out. Once that was done, Newf Friends would arrange for one of their volunteers to come to my house and do an in-person assessment to make sure I had an appropriate home and yard and was a suitable, responsible owner. If all that went smoothly, a trip to the foster home to meet the dog would be arranged, and at that point, if I was sure I wanted him, I'd be able to take him home with me.

It all happened very fast. I filled out and returned the paperwork as soon as it arrived in mid January. The in-person assessment was scheduled a few days later. I had nothing to hide, but I was nervous, deeply afraid I'd be judged unfit. For the first time in months I cleaned up my house. It took me days. There were weeks' worth of empty pizza boxes, beer bottles, dirty pots and pans and dirty laundry scattered throughout the house. Instead of washing any dishes, I had gone out and bought disposable paper plates and plastic knives and forks—except I didn't dispose of them. My place looked like a bad episode of that TV show about hoarders. But now I threw out bags and bags of trash. I swept and I scrubbed. I found clothes I thought I had lost. When things were in order, I felt much better. This dog was helping me already and he wasn't even here yet.

When the day came for the home inspection and interview, I paced at the front window, awaiting the volunteer's arrival. I was tense. I smoked a few cigarettes, trying to calm down. Then I panicked—if she saw that I smoked, maybe she would be concerned. I threw the half-full pack of cigarettes into the garbage. Then sprayed a full bottle of Febreze into the air. If nothing else, the place now smelled great. I felt like I was going on a first date, and wanted to impress this woman but really had no clue how to do it. I was nervous and sweaty. Who was I kidding? I wouldn't let a dog live with me.

The woman who arrived was sweet and soft-spoken. For years at work I'd often met with CEOs and vice presidents of some of the biggest and most powerful corporations on the planet and had never felt nervous, but I was inexplicably anxious in this woman's presence. I was sure she'd find out there was something terribly wrong, something that made me unsuitable to take on the responsibility of owning a dog.

I walked her around the house and out into the backyard while she asked me a string of questions: "What's your work flexibility? What is a typical day like for you? Do you have family or friends who have dogs? Do you travel for work? Do you have the time to exercise a dog twice a day?" I stammered out answers as best I could, and she noted them on her clipboard.

"If your dog was injured, what would be the first thing you'd do?"

"That would be pretty upsetting, but I have had lots of first-aid training. I would calm him and reassure him, and get him to a vet as quickly as possible."

"Do you know where the closest vets are?" she asked.

I did! Most definitely. In fact, I'd given this great thought and had actually done some research beforehand to find out. But for a moment it was like I was a kid in an exam, and my mind went blank. Then I remembered the name and address of one vet and blurted it out, loudly . . . or so it seemed.

"Great," she said, and scribbled something down. "If you were saving money for a vacation and your dog needed a medical procedure, would you get the procedure or go on vacation?"

Well, if the dog wanted a facelift for those droopy eyes, I wasn't quite sure what I'd do, but I said, "I would always prioritize my dog's health over my vacation plans. No question."

"Do you know," she said, "that Newfoundland dogs have a particular affinity for water?"

"Yes," I said. "I do know. And so do I, actually." I told her that I grew up in Nova Scotia by the ocean, that I was a surfer, a former life-guard and competitive swimmer, and a former coach. I explained that I thought raising a dog—especially one coming from difficult circum-stances—might be a little like being a coach, requiring a similar blend of patience, support and encouragement.

"Very true," she said as we put our coats on before heading outside to the nearby park. "But," she added, "you'd be surprised how quickly the roles reverse."

"How so?" I asked.

She smiled at me in a funny way and then headed out the door, with me following closely behind her.

We walked to the park across the street and watched a group of dogs chasing each other through the snow, as their owners huddled together, holding on to their cups of Starbucks as their only source of heat. "These are the dogs I think he'd play with," I told her.

She clearly liked the fact that the park was so near my house.

"So, how did this dog end up in this situation, needing to be adopted?" I inquired. "Does he have behavioral issues or anything I should be concerned about?"

A serious look crept over her face. "He has had a difficult time, but from what we have seen at his foster home, it's through no fault of his own." She paused, letting that sink in. "We have seen a lot of sad cases. Some people aren't prepared to care for a dog like a Newfoundland. They are big, they tend to shed a lot, some drool excessively and they are devoted to their owners and need to be around them constantly. Some call them 'Velcro dogs' because they always want to stick close by. It makes some people uncomfortable and they can't manage that."

I nodded, trying to picture a big dog following me around the house.

"Some people think that because they are so big, they would be

ideal guard dogs, but in fact they are extremely gentle. As a result, some are neglected or abused, in a misguided attempt to make them mean and aggressive. The owner gets frustrated, the dog becomes scared, and it isn't a good ending. I really can't tell you that much about Kong's exact circumstance. However, what we do know, and what is most important, is that he lacks confidence. He hasn't had the attention he needs, and he was left alone, abandoned in a terrible way. He will need patience. The best thing to help this dog is that you treat him kindly and give him lots of affection. Despite their size, these dogs are sensitive and will respond to kindness more than anything else."

She stopped walking and faced me. "You have a nice house and this is a great park for him, but do you have the patience to help him live a happy life?"

At that moment I didn't even know if I had the patience to let myself live a happy life, let alone a big, neglected dog. I glanced down at the snow and took a few steps. "That's a fair question," I said as I gathered my thoughts. "I can only imagine that I would be patient enough to give him a happy life because we both want the same thing. I would try very hard to provide him with the best care possible and do whatever it takes to make sure he is looked after properly. I certainly don't need a guard dog, but it would be nice to have a companion to share the house with. I would take very good care of him."

"If you were here in the park and he was misbehaving and wouldn't respond to you, would you ever use force as a form of discipline?"

Force as a form of discipline. I was definitely not a fan. I'd learned as a child that force of any kind, even verbal, can leave scars, not always the kind you can see. And I'd always admired my grandfather for his incredible patience and kindness, two qualities that made my childhood much better and showed me there were other ways to manage situations.

"Force as a form of discipline is not a method I condone or would

ever use. It might be effective in the moment, but long term, I feel it only causes resentment."

"Yes, I think that's true," she said, jotting down my answer on her clipboard.

"If he attacked another dog or was trying to bolt into the street or something, I'd definitely try to restrain him—just to stop him from getting hurt—but I'd never hit a dog under any circumstances." She glanced up from her clipboard long enough to give me an encouraging nod.

"Do you realize this dog might not be able or willing to listen to all commands at the beginning?"

"Look," I said. "I don't expect him to respond to me right away, or for him and me to be instant best friends. In view of what he's gone through, I think kindness and patience will probably be the best thing for him, and I promise you—and him—that I'll be nothing but gentle, even in challenging situations. I think that if he sees over time that I'm the guy who feeds him, takes him out for walks and gives him affection, he'll come around. I hope that with time we'll make a connection. I am very committed to this—that's why I called you. I don't want to waste your time or mine, so I need you to know that I would provide him with the best home possible."

She bowed her head and put her pen away. Interview over.

We returned to the house in silence. She asked to use the phone privately and left me in the living room for a few minutes. When she came back into the room, she was smiling.

"I just called the head of Newf Friends to go over our discussion," she said. "You answered our questions very well. You have a really nice house, beautifully suited to dog ownership, and you seem like a kind, responsible person. We think that this dog could do quite well with you and hope you'll choose to adopt him."

I smiled broadly for the first time in months. And for the first time in months I was excited.

PART TWO

Rescue

FIVE

I drove up to the foster home the next weekend, on a Saturday in late January. I was glad to have a purpose, rather than sitting in the house speculating about Jane. I was going to see the dog! Maybe *my* dog! The drive was a good two-plus hours in ideal conditions, so my plan was to get out the door by mid morning, but when I woke up to a full-fledged snowstorm, I knew I was in for a long day, no matter what time I left. I dressed, and ate breakfast, then got in the car and picked my way carefully out of the downtown core and along the highway through the suburbs west of the city. It was slow going and the visibility wasn't great, but the road had seen a plow in the not-too-distant past and I could make out the lane markings.

Well, sort of seen a plow. The right lane had been "plowed" by the passage of cars ahead of me, leaving only tire ruts in snow to mark the path ahead. Of course that path was nearly impossible to see, what with the endless snow blowing straight at my windshield. Most of the time, I was looking out into an unbroken wall of white. Every now and then I would come up behind a transport truck kicking up a massive, powdery rooster tail and be forced to pass the vehicle, which meant pulling into the untended left lane and leaving my fate in God's hands.

If you've driven on a four-lane highway in a snowstorm, you know all too well this scene and the tension that accompanies it. When I finally exited the highway, the snow let up a bit, but the layer that had already fallen was still sitting several inches thick on the smaller country roads and I could feel the car intermittently lose its grip and drift sideways in short fishtails. After more than three hours of white-knuckle driving, I found the place. It was situated in a field next to a barn and had a long laneway that led in from the road. I still had both hands on the wheel and hadn't relaxed my grip, but when I turned into the lane and saw him, I felt the full weight of the drive melt away.

He was perched at the top of a hill where the laneway ended about eighty yards from the snow-covered dirt road I'd turned off. He was just standing there, looking down the driveway, as I slowly approached in my car. He was all by himself, the snow piled up at his feet and drifting down onto his big, black head, yet he didn't look the least bit cold. As I turned into the lane, he didn't bark or rush the car; he just stood and watched. He was stunning, truly a beautiful dog, unlike any other dog I had ever seen in person or in pictures. I couldn't take my eyes off him. From his nose to the tip of his tail, he was well over six feet long—a massive animal—and there were two black splotches, on his right flank and at the base of his tail, that hadn't been visible in the photo online.

He held his head with dignity, like a king, and he looked pensive and curious. His big, droopy eyes were intelligent and aware. In the flesh he was imposing; with his size and his distinctive markings and the way he held himself, he seemed larger than life. It was like coming across a celebrity by accident. At first, as you notice someone you've only seen in pictures or on TV moving about in your normal world, doing normal things, you can't quite believe your eyes. You try not to stare or make a big deal, but inside you're excited. That's how

I felt when I first saw this dog. He watched me as I drove by, and once I was about twenty feet ahead, I looked into the rearview mirror and saw him jogging up behind the car, his long, shaggy coat shedding snow as he went.

The house was a red-brick square, with an addition built off the front. It stood beside the worn but sturdy barn. There was a plowed parking area between the house and barn, and I pulled into it. A halogen light on a hydro pole gave off a halo of fuzzy blue illumination as the snow continued to fall.

It turned out my Newf wasn't the only dog on the premises—not by a long stretch. As I got out of the car, a whole pack descended on me, all of them barking and chasing each other. There was another Newfoundland—this one all black—a German shepherd and a pair of mutts whose breeds were impossible to determine. All four ranked among the biggest dogs I'd ever seen, and they crowded around me in a flurry of wagging tails and licking tongues. All of them, that is, except my Newf.

Coming in from the lane behind me, he watched from afar. He didn't bolt when I exited the car; he just stood back at a safe distance and cautiously observed. At one point the German shepherd broke free of the pack and ran over to him. They sniffed each other and ran around a bit. But when the other dog turned and headed back over to me, my Newf stayed where he was.

"He's a little leery of men," a voice called out from behind me. "He's going to take some work." I turned and saw a woman bundled up in a thick winter jacket and a tuque walking toward me from the house. This must be the lady who is fostering him, I thought. I smiled at her and said hello.

The pack broke away from me and ran to her as she approached. In stride, she delivered a few quick pats before the dogs changed

direction again and headed off toward the barn. At the edge of the parking area there was a freestanding feed trough with a running tap at the edge and they stopped at it to lap up water. My Newf turned his attention from me and joined the pack to have a drink.

A small girl, who looked about eight years old and was even more bundled up than her mother, leaped out the front door and tore off into the snow toward the dogs. She ran headlong into the pack at the trough and they immediately started to play with her, rolling around in the snow; however, my Newf slowly backed away from the action.

"How is he with kids?" I asked.

"He's gentle," she answered. "He runs away a bit at first, but when they aren't quite so rambunctious, he relaxes. It just takes him a while."

She hadn't had him long, only two or three weeks, as he'd been in another foster home prior to hers. She didn't know much about his original owners. He'd arrived underfed and a bit underweight. Even though his fur was thick, I could now see it hung large on him, like a coat that was a few sizes too big.

"He's terrified of loud noises. He doesn't like it when the kids yell," the woman said. "And he cowers if anyone makes sudden movements around him, so you have to be a bit careful that he doesn't get spooked. I'm not sure he assumes he's going to be petted when someone comes close, you know?" she said.

She didn't offer up any more information than that, but she did say that one of his original owners had gotten him hoping he'd make an intimidating guard dog. She assumed that when he didn't display the aggression they desired, they got rid of him. He had bounced around with several owners, none of whom really wanted him.

"The details of what happened to him in the past are not nearly as important as what is going to happen to him in the future," she said. "That's why our rescue organization tries as hard as we do to find these

gentle giants homes where they will be well cared for and respected and loved." She turned to look me in the eye. "All he wants is a warm, safe place to sleep, some food in his belly and someone to love him."

I yearned to rescue this big, beautiful dog, but given everything that had recently happened in my life, maybe I was taking on more than I could handle. I suddenly felt a little pressure and a lot of responsibility. I studied the big guy as he stood in the snow cautiously studying me. What was he thinking? And what was I thinking?

"He's good with women," she told me. "He warms up to them right away."

"But not men," I said.

"Not at first, and he seems particularly scared of taller men," she said. "I'll see if I can call him over and you can introduce yourself, but try not to loom over him. Get down to his level and move really slowly, so you don't scare him."

We both crouched and she called out his name, "Kong! Come!" She explained that this was the temporary name her daughter had given him because he was as big as King Kong. "You don't have to call him that," she assured me. "Actually, it's best if you choose your own name for him, one that you feel suits him."

He started over readily enough, but slowed when he saw me and stopped entirely about ten feet away, closer to her than to me. "I don't think he'll walk right up to you," she said. "But he should be okay if you go to him. Just stay low."

Leaning over, my knees bent, I moved towards him as slowly as I could. He hadn't seemed aggressive when playing with the other dogs, so I wasn't worried about him biting me, but he was just so big, and I was concerned that my nervousness would scare him off. "There, there, big guy. It's okay," I said. "I'm just coming over to say hello." He backed up a little when I got near, but he didn't run.

Up close, he was awe inspiring. I was astonished by how self-possessed he seemed. He gazed right into my eyes in the most extraordinary way, a look that revealed intelligence but also wide-eyed caution. And there was something else. Even though he was young (they had estimated he was between one and two years old), he had the eyes of an old soul, the same eyes I'd seen in the Petfinder photo.

I carefully held my hand out to him. His muzzle moved from side to side a foot from my hand, taking in my scent. When he didn't growl or edge away, I inched closer, bit by bit, until the back of my hand was right in front of his nose.

He was on high alert, hardly moving. I could see the whites of his giant, unblinking eyes. His head hung low, but he seemed determined not to show his fear too much. He continued to look me straight in the eye as I got closer, and held our eye contact, unlike any dog I'd ever met. It was as if he wanted me to know he was appraising me as much as I was him and he was going to set his own terms. Despite whatever neglect or abuse he'd suffered, he still had that dignity in him. I felt his whiskers brush my fingers as he took in my scent. He was staring up at me, his big, brown eyes saying, "I want to like you, but I'm just not sure." I didn't try to pet him, just withdrew my hand once he'd backed his muzzle away. We looked at each other awhile longer and then I moved away from him and stood up.

Calling her daughter and dogs after us, the woman led me into her house. Inside, a very necessary mudroom opened into the living room. The dogs poured in after us, tracking snow everywhere. "I just let it go during the day," the woman told me, nodding at the mess. "Before I go to bed, I get a mop out and clean it all up. The foster dogs usually aren't with me long enough for me to teach them any manners."

The all-black Newfoundland, the dog that had been friendliest, belonged to the family. Extremely sweet-tempered, she was the spark

that had convinced the woman to start fostering in the first place. She loved the breed deeply and used her dog as an example of how Kong might eventually act once he opened up to me. We had a cup of coffee and talked as I watched Kong move around the house. He filled the room with his presence.

Before meeting him, my main concern was that he might be aggressive toward people or other dogs. Now, however, seeing him in person, I knew that aggression wouldn't be an issue. But his size would. This was an enormous dog. Could I handle him if he had a mind of his own? I had no earthly idea. Here, in this rural setting, he had lots of room to himself, and it was really quiet and serene. But what if he bolted once he got to the city? What if traffic scared him? And what about the regular noise of an urban center? What would I do with this massive terrified dog then if it was all too much for him?

I had promised myself that I wouldn't bring him home after only one visit—I wanted to make sure I didn't rush into anything. But at some point in the two hours I spent watching him, and despite all the voices in my head saying, "Don't do it!" I found myself announcing, "I would like to take him home with me today."

"Today?" the woman repeated.

"Today. Yes. If that's okay. He is beautiful, and he seems very sweet and gentle. I think I can give him a good home." I looked over at the big dog, now lying in the corner, watching me. "Once in a while in life we all need someone to help look after us. Might as well start now."

"I agree," she said. "And I have a feeling he could become a very good dog someday."

There was a bit of paperwork to fill out. I sat down at the kitchen table to take care of it, and while I did, the woman walked my dog—my stunning black-and-white Newfoundland—outside to relieve himself before the drive to the city. When we'd both finished our respective

business, she gave me a short leash and a collar and helped me load him into the backseat of my car. He was a little hesitant, but she coaxed him and he gently stepped into my car. I got in after he was settled, and when I rolled down the window to say goodbye, the woman leaned in and gave me one last bit of advice. "If, for whatever reason, it doesn't work out, please call us and we will take him back," she began. "But you should give it some time if you can. It's traumatic every time a dog changes homes. He won't turn into the perfect pet in one day. Be patient. Wait, just wait." Funny she said that, because my grandfather used to say the same thing to my brother and me when we were kids: "Wait a bit. Just wait a bit. Try not to rush so much. Do things properly, and good things will come your way."

I nodded and thanked her, rolled up the window and set off for home.

As we pulled out of the driveway and onto the road, I glanced back to make sure he was okay. I was leveled by the sheer size of him. He took up the entire backseat. It reminded me of that scene in the movie *Jaws* when they see the shark for the first time and Roy Scheider says, "We're going to need a bigger boat." I was going to need a bigger car.

As nervous as Kong had been earlier in the day, he didn't cower or whimper. He sat quietly, staring straight ahead out the windshield. I looked back at the woman and her daughter and waved as we drove away. I was surprised that the dog didn't look back. He had his sight only on what lay ahead. I couldn't help but think of Jane the night she left: she never looked back, either.

As I drove, a million thoughts raced through my mind. Where was this dog going to sleep? What if he barked and drove the neighbors crazy? What kind of food did he like? But the refrain my mind kept coming back to was "Oh my god. I just adopted a 140-pound dog. What the hell am I doing?"

The other thing bugging me was the name the foster family had given this animal. Kong. Aside from the fact that he was big, it didn't suit him at all. It was a novelty name, as though he was a carnival attraction or some sort of freak show. I could not bring myself to call him that. The question was, what would his name be?

"What are we going to call you, big guy?" I said, glancing at him in the rearview mirror. He kept quiet the whole way, gazing straight ahead out the window.

SIX

Two hours later, on a drive back that was much easier than the way there but filled with a different kind of tension due to my new companion in the rear, we were home. Or at least, I was home. The leviathan in the backseat was in a very strange land, one filled with brightly shining lights, tightly packed houses and fast-moving vehicles. He didn't bark or make a sound, but his head was on a swivel the second we approached the city.

Instead of pulling around the back and into the garage, I parked in front of my house. I stopped in almost the exact spot Jane had when she'd told me she was leaving me. It was the first time I'd parked there since she'd left. I turned the car off and pivoted to the dog in the backseat. His giant head was now lowered and he looked up at me with his big brown eyes as if to say, "Please don't hurt me." For the first time since the whole "get a dog" urge started, I felt sad. I felt sorry for this creature. What if I couldn't make him feel safe and secure? If I couldn't do it for myself, how was I going to do it for him?

"It's okay, big guy. I won't hurt you," I said a few times, as I slowly reached out to let him smell my hand. He let me gently rub his ears, but his apprehension never wavered. "Let's take you to the park. I bet

you have to pee." It was a phrase I would say over and over in the days, weeks, months and years ahead.

I lowered the front seat of my two-door sports coupe, quite possibly the worst car I could have for such a big dog, and tightly wrapped the leash Newf Friends had provided around my hand. "Let's go, big guy. Let's go for our first walk." I motioned toward the open door and he leaned forward, his enormous nose twitching as he smelled the air of a city for the first time. A minute or so later, he put one awkward paw down on the floor of the backseat, followed by another down on the road. He cautiously glanced around and then hopped onto the street. Then he gazed up at me. "Good boy! See, you're okay. Let's go."

I led him across the street and into the park. To be perfectly honest, I'm not sure who was leading who. He wasn't totally unman-ageable, but clearly he wasn't used to walking on a leash, and he basically moved from smell to smell, dragging me along behind him. Eventually he stopped by a light pole and sniffed frantically while circling the pole, and then took an astonishingly long pee—a solid fifteen or twenty seconds. I hadn't seen racehorses pee that much, never mind a dog. This was followed by more pulling and sniffing across the snow-covered ground, where he suddenly stopped and then squatted, producing my first glimpse of yet another reality of owning a giant dog. I had a plastic bag with me (thank goodness it was a grocery bag, not those tiny ones they sell at pet stores), and as I stooped to clean up after him, the question came to me again: "What the hell am I doing with you?" I asked it out loud as I attempted to veer this leviathan of a dog toward a garbage can so I could get rid of the perilously full bag. He kept walking in tangents, almost pulling me off my feet to track scents in the snow. I am six-foot-one, weigh 210 pounds and have taken my share of body checks, knocks and bumps playing hockey. But my walk in the park with this dog was

anything but a "walk in the park." Despite being underweight, this dog was incredibly strong.

"Hey!" I pulled back on the leash and tried to get his attention. He stopped for a second to turn around, giving me a look that said, "What do you want?" Progress! I'd finally caught his attention. But before I could be too pleased with myself, off he went in another direction, hauling me behind him.

The big dog dragged me around the park a bit more, until I eventually veered us toward my house. It was getting cold and starting to snow even more, and it was time to introduce him to his new home. "Here we are, big guy," I said, as we made our way up the short walk to the front door. I looked down at him, hoping he would give me a happy bark and eagerly wag his tail like on those *Lassie* episodes I watched as a kid. Instead he stopped dead in his tracks, immovable as a rock.

"C'mon. It's time. It's going to be okay," I said. Reluctantly he followed me up the three stairs onto the front porch, and I told him to sit as I fumbled with my keys. Naturally he didn't sit. Instead he stood motionless and unsure as I opened the door. "This is it. This is your new home."

He eyed me as if to say, "What am I supposed to do?"

"All right. I'll go first," I said, crossing the threshold. "It's totally safe. Come." And with that, we were in the foyer. But no sooner had I said it was safe than I tripped over the hockey bag I'd left at the door. I didn't fall, but my lunge startled the poor dog and he cowered on the floor. "I'm sorry," I said gently. "You're okay. I just lost my balance."

I was met with a very unsure look. I sat down on the floor beside the enormous ball of fur and slowly unclipped the leash. "Everything is okay. You can walk around, check it out . . . Just don't pee in here." It was a joke, but I wasn't joking—not that he got it.

Since I had promised myself I wouldn't bring a dog home on a first visit, I hadn't done anything to dog-proof the house. My place hadn't

seen a mop or broom since the volunteer had been there to check it out, and the empty food containers had made a return appearance in almost all the rooms on the first floor. I got up and started tidying.

I kept an eye on the big dog as I cleaned old pizza boxes and Chinese-food containers, empty juice boxes and beer bottles. He crept from the entranceway into the living room, cautiously sniffing at the floor and the furniture. For such a giant creature, he could pad along so delicately. As I kept tabs on him, he did the same with me, tracking my movements out of the corner of an eye and avoiding me as best he could. If I moved more than about six feet near him, he'd back away. It was as if we were both magnetized to maintain the same distance between us at all times.

In the confines of my home, he seemed even more massive, and every time he entered a room it felt full to capacity. Trying to open things up for him, I shifted around some of the furniture, while he explored the new space with his head lowered and his nose working overtime.

Just when he was calming down and moving along with a bit more purpose, a loud ring of my cell phone caused him to jump and hide under the dining room table—which, of course, was smaller than he was. I grabbed my phone quickly and turned off the ringer as I checked who it was: Matt, no doubt calling to ask how the visit to the foster home went. I'd call him back later. Now I needed to coax the giant out from under the table. "It's only a cell phone," I said. "It's not scary." I held the phone up for him to see. He met my gaze, but his body language said, "Stay back," so I did. I went to the living room and sat down. I turned on the TV, with the volume on low. He eventually settled and lay on the floor, watching me from afar. This would take some time, and I needed to be patient, I reminded myself.

And that's when I realized I was so ill-prepared that I didn't even have any dog food. With the basic cleanup out of the way, I decided to

make a run to a pet store, and because I didn't want to leave the dog alone in the house by himself quite yet, I had to bring him with me.

At the farm I'd had the foster woman's help in putting the leash on him, and the only other time I'd had to get it on him he was in the tight confines of the backseat of my car. Now I got down low and inched my way over to him, holding the leash out in front of me. "Time to go for another short car ride," I said. "You must be hungry." He was teetering on the edge of flight, and if he could have run away from me, he would have, but there was nowhere for him to go. Reluctantly, his head down, and eyeing me suspiciously the whole time, he let me clip the leash to his collar and we headed out the door. It was so obvious he didn't want to go, but what was I supposed to do? I got him outside and opened the car door to invite him in. He jumped onto the backseat with a bit of coaxing.

With my new dog staring out the window and taking in all the sights, I drove to a big-box pet store. Dogs were allowed in the store, which was great, but as we walked in, I started to doubt whether arriving with a dog clearly not socialized very much was such a good idea. The second we entered he was overloaded with dog-friendly sights and smells. It was probably his first time in a store like this, and he was like a kid at Christmas. He started pulling me straight to the rawhide dog bones, smartly displayed at dog height. He grabbed one before I could say or do anything to stop him. As I firmly said, "No," and began to gently pull the toy out of his mouth, he abandoned the rawhide bone and lurched toward a huge, plush donut. Once it was lodged in his jaws, he started pulling me down the aisle again. I noticed people staring. It was somewhat embarrassing to be yanked down aisle after aisle by a giant, donut-carrying dog.

Thankfully a store employee intervened. "You look like you might need some help," she said. I wasn't even going to try and be cool. I just nodded a desperate yes.

"What a beautiful dog he is. What's his name?" I quickly explained that he was a rescue and I had just gotten him, and he didn't have a name yet. Meanwhile, Kong sat down calmly beside the woman, donut still in his mouth, and let her rub his head. The lady at the farm had been right: he absolutely was more comfortable around women than men.

Some other customers in the store had stopped shopping and were watching what was rapidly becoming a spectacle. I tried to get back to business. "I'm wondering if you can help me choose some basic things—a food dish, a water bowl, a good-quality food, some treats . . . And I guess we're taking that giant donut," I said, noting how much saliva was now on it.

"Sure thing," she replied. "Why don't I hold his leash." I handed it over to her and she looked down at the big dog and said, "Come with me, beautiful boy." With that, Kong followed her over to the leash-and-collar section, with me lagging behind. She picked out a collar (the biggest one they carried) and fitted it onto him easily. Kong obviously liked having the salesgirl close to him, and I was pretty sure he would never have let me put anything around his neck the way he let her do it.

"Give that a try," she said, passing me the leash. I followed her through the store, and although Kong tried hurling me down the aisles, the new collar definitely helped me control him better. When we got to the food selection, I said, "He's still far too thin, and I'm looking for a really good food that will help him put on weight."

"Of course," the woman said. "I've got a couple of choices that would be just right." She carefully explained the options and I chose a big bag of premium food that had high protein content, organic ingredients and was free of fillers. Next we picked out a big stainless-steel water bowl and matching food bowl. I also thought he should have his own bed, a warm, soft place to sleep. The problem was, despite an entire row full of them there weren't many that were big enough. In fact, only one

was Newf sized, and it looked (and cost) the same as a Sealy Posturepedic. I took it off the shelf and put it on the floor.

"Come. Have a seat on your new bed."

He didn't even glance at it.

"He's probably too distracted to lie down," the woman said, trying to make me feel better. "But I'm sure he'll use it in your house," she added. "And it's really sweet that you want him to have a nice bed."

Together we picked it up and hauled it to the checkout. Here's the crazy thing: I couldn't fit the bed into the small trunk of my car, so I had to jam it in the backseat then ask the dog, who was already cautious about the tight confines, to sit on top of it. He refused to get in the back, leaving me with no choice but to let him sit in the front. Once I opened the passenger door, he climbed in and stared straight ahead. His head was above mine and almost touched the roof of the car. We looked ridiculous, like a comical circus act. I prayed that we didn't get stopped by the police on our way home. Fortunately my prayers were answered.

Back at the house, I left the bed in the front hall after he walked right past it into the living room. I brought the bowls into the kitchen, filled one with water and set it just outside the doorway. He was lying at the far end of the living room, watching me, his head on the floor, tucked between his front paws. His eyebrows were up, and his big, droopy eyes were alert. Still, I couldn't quite read the meaning of his body language. If dogs could play cards, he would be an excellent poker player.

"You thirsty?" I asked, still crouched by the water bowl.

Silence.

"You hungry?"

No reaction.

I went back out to the hallway and grabbed the bag of food. In the kitchen, I cut it open and found a beat-up mug waiting to be reborn

as a dog-food scoop. I filled the bowl and then gingerly padded into the living room with it. "Time for dinner," I said, giving the bowl a shake. He tensed at the sound, as though preparing to get up and run. I'd never heard of a dog able to resist the sound of kibble hitting the bowl—but this dog was different. I put the bowl on the floor. Then I walked a few paces backward to give him some space. "Go ahead," I said. "You can eat now."

He remained motionless.

I waited . . . and waited. Then waited some more. The dog fixed me with a stare that said, "No way. Not a chance." It was as if I'd put a box of nails on the floor rather than a bowl of tasty food. I waited a little longer and then relented. "Okay. Fine. Have it your way. I'll just leave the bowl there and you can eat it when you want to." I went into the kitchen again. And only when my back was turned while I searched for a place to store the dog's food did I hear the sound of those giant paws, crossing the living room floor and stopping. Pause. A few seconds later, the telltale sound: the crunching of kibble. Music to my ears. I stood stock-still, listening, afraid that if I closed a cupboard door too loud or moved around, I'd spook him and he would stop eating.

As I stood there listening, I thought of Jane, who loved dogs. I knew she'd adore him on sight. And I had to wonder if, unlike me, she'd have an instant rapport with him the way she did with pretty much everyone she met. In fact, the first time I'd encountered the Newfoundland breed was with her on our honeymoon. We were in Paris and had gone to visit the Eiffel Tower. In the park at the base of the tower, an elderly woman was walking a gently swaying mountain of black fur. Jane was totally taken by the dog and we rushed over to talk to the owner. For ten minutes we butchered the French language as we both knelt and patted the majestic animal. He was gentle and affectionate, leaning against our legs and into our hands. Jane was so

moved she grabbed my arm and gazed up at me with a bright expression that said, "Isn't this one of the most beautiful dogs you have ever seen?" Maybe if I called her and told her I got a dog, she'd— I cut myself off before finishing the hopeless thought. I carefully tucked the bag of food away in a cupboard and quietly closed the door.

Out in the living room I could still hear *crunch—crunch—crunch*. I couldn't resist any longer. I tiptoed to the entranceway and peeked in. The sound stopped before I'd even cleared the door frame. He was lying down in front of his bowl. He turned his face up to me with a look of apprehension.

"Sorry," I said, excusing myself. Why won't he eat in front of me? I wondered. But at least he's eating.

Or was. As I went back into the kitchen and set about making a dinner of my own, I heard him get up and walk away from the bowl.

I heated up some leftovers and ventured back into the living room with my meal. "Okay if I come in now?" He was lying in a corner of the room, fully alert, head up and chest out. Maybe he wasn't ready to eat in front of me, but I was going to eat in front of him. I could feel his eyes on me as I brought the fork to my mouth, but every time I looked at him, he looked away. After I'd had a few bites he got up and left the room. Another dinner alone, I told myself.

There was something deeply disturbing to me about this behavior. What would make a dog feel afraid of eating in front of a human being? The answers that came to my head made me feel even more concerned about the treatment this animal might have received.

As I ate my meal, I listened to Kong padding around the first floor of the house, exploring it without me. It was astonishing. He had only been a part of my life for a few hours, yet everything felt different. Even when he wasn't in my line of sight, the mood in the house was different. It was . . . no longer empty. It was occupied. It was full. Full of life.

Which isn't to say it was entirely comfortable. There was some tension and a bit of apprehension between this new arrival and me. Still, it was exciting to feel his presence and it was nice to have something, anything, to get excited about. For the first time since Jane left, I had company. And it felt great.

When I was done eating, I grabbed the dog bed from the front entrance, carried it upstairs and laid it in a corner of my bedroom. I called for the dog to come up and see it, which felt a bit strange because I didn't have a name for him yet. He moved to the bottom of the stairs and gazed up at me but wouldn't climb them.

"Come on, buddy. Come on up." He glanced around, took a step or two, but then lowered his head and stopped. I descended the stairs and he backed up to keep that same distance between us. I got his leash from where I'd hung it beside the door and walked over to him. He let me get it back on him and lead him upstairs. When we made it to the top, I said, "Welcome to the second floor," and eased off the leash.

At first he didn't move.

"You can look around. Don't mind the mess."

He put his nose to the floor and took a sniff. Then he slowly walked from the landing into the hall. I moved into my bedroom and settled myself on my bed, listening as he sniffed around the bathroom and guest bedroom. Eventually I saw a huge head appear in the doorway of my room. "Hey, big guy," I said. "This is the bedroom. You can hang out here any time you want."

He sniffed the air like he was searching for clues. I was fascinated by how much his nose twitched.

"Do you want to lie down in your new bed? It's nicer than mine, so if you don't like it, we can trade." He didn't get my sense of humor and stared at me, aloof, unreadable. I would have given a lot of money to know what was going through his mind at that moment.

After a while he went back downstairs, and I followed him down a minute or two later.

The rest of the night played out in slow motion. I was so absorbed with him that every tiny movement seemed significant. I called Matt back at some point.

"I don't know, Matt," I said. "I think things are okay, but I don't know if he likes me much."

"Can you blame him?" Matt quipped.

"Thanks, pal."

"Relax. Things will be fine. Just don't smother him and say 'I'm your best friend, I'm your best friend.'"

Was that what I was doing? Maybe. Probably. Yeah.

"Let him draw his own conclusions in his own time," Matt said. "That's what I let you do when I suggested you get a dog. You took your time and figured it out. He'll ultimately do the same thing."

It was good advice. Being overly attentive would only stress him out. But this logic went against every fiber of my being. I saw a creature that was scared and upset, and all I wanted to do was hug him and reassure him he would be okay from now on.

"All right, Matt," I said. "Thanks."

"No problem. See you at the office."

After I hung up I talked myself out of going to see what the dog was doing and turned on the TV, instead. A few minutes later there he was at the entrance. He looked at me once, then entered the room and lay down on the opposite side. I sat on the floor, not the couch, hoping he'd come over to me. He didn't. We stayed like that for a while. At one point I got up to get a glass of water and he jumped out of his skin.

"It's okay, it's okay! Ev-v-verything's okay." Of course I said it way too loud—and only made matters worse.

I came back with my water and the dog paced for a while. Then

that giant head appeared at the threshold yet again. My Newf crossed it and took up a new place in the living room, cautiously lowering himself as though he wasn't sure it was safe.

"You can sit wherever you want," I said. I watched him in place of whatever show was on and eventually he fell asleep. Even asleep he seemed uneasy. His back legs were tucked under him and his head was resting on his front paws. Here was a dog that was physically imposing, with an uncommon beauty and presence, but meeting basic needs eluded him: how to eat, who to trust, when and where to sleep. Even when he was asleep, all I wanted to do was reach out and hug him. But I didn't.

Instead I went up to bed. He didn't follow me. I whistled for him from my room. He didn't come. But after an hour or so, I heard the click of his nails at the bottom of the stairs and then heard him start to climb them. A moment later he appeared in my bedroom doorway. "Hey there, big guy," I said. "Come on in."

He entered the room, head down, swaying sweetly and looking up at me as though peering over the top of a pair of reading glasses—an expression I would later come to regard as one of his defining mannerisms. He walked past his expensive dog bed to the corner of the room opposite his bed and flopped down on the hard floor. It was a breakthrough. I wanted to rush over and tell him what a good boy he was, but I didn't. I stayed perfectly still, smiling to myself with the sheets pulled under my chin. And at some point, we both fell asleep.

SEVEN

He was still there when I woke up in the morning. "Hey," I called to him. "Hey, buddy." He was alert, but he stayed put and watched me as I got out of bed and walked his way. I bent over, extending my hand so he could sniff it. After a few seconds he let me move closer, and I gently rubbed his head. "So, did you have a good sleep?" He appeared less tense than he had the day before, but his eyes were still wide and cautious. "Ready for a morning walk?"

I went down the stairs and a minute or so later I heard the big dog make his way down. I got bundled up and then slowly clipped his leash on him, which he let me do without backing away. We went out for a walk, with me waiting in the cold while he sniffed at bushes, poles and trees, found the spots he liked and composed his messages to the world. He didn't know how to walk on a leash any more than I knew how to steer him. He pulled me around from smell to smell. A few other dog owners observed the spectacle with raised eyebrows, but all in all, our second walk was successful. No broken bones and no runaway dog. At this early stage, that felt like an accomplishment.

"Well done, big guy," I said, as I unlocked the front door. Once we were back in the warm house, he continued his inspection of his

new environment. I filled his bowl with food and called him over, shaking the bowl so he could hear it was full. He stopped to eye me as I lowered the bowl to the kitchen floor, but he did not approach. "Here's your breakfast," I added cheerily, like I was a diner waitress looking for a big tip. I have friends with dogs that jump with excitement when their food is poured, as though mealtime is the most exciting moment of the day. Not this guy. Nothing. Not even a tiny tail wag. Just two big, inscrutable eyes staring at me.

"Okay. Suit yourself. It will be there when you are hungry," I said. Then I went upstairs to shower. When I came back downstairs a few minutes later, he was standing almost in the same spot. His head was lowered and his big brown eyes were regarding me apprehensively. "What? What happened?" I asked, and then I noticed that half the food was missing from his bowl. I said, "Good boy. Eating is good. That's what you're supposed to do. Good, good boy." Yet those wary eyes didn't change.

We spent the rest of the day, a cold and quiet winter Sunday, inside the house, moving around each other. I tried several times to coax him to sit beside me, but he eyed me as if to say, "I'm fine where I am, thanks." I couldn't take it personally. Even as he kept his distance, the same feelings I'd had the night before filled my chest: that it was so pleasant having him in the house and he was such good company, even if he was a bit aloof. Once again I acknowledged that the place was no longer empty, and instead of dwelling on Jane's absence, I was thinking about this dog. It was a marked change for me, as different and foreign as it must have been for the big dog lying on my floor.

I decided to invite a friend over to meet my new dog. When she arrived, I was reading in the living room, with the dog off in a far corner. She knocked on the door, and that's when I heard him bark for the first time—a deep, incredibly loud bark—and I nearly jumped

out of my own skin. "Jeezus that's loud!" I said to myself as my heart pounded like a jackhammer. Kong and I both got up and walked toward the front door. He stopped after a few steps and then stared up at me. For the first time I noticed a slight wag of his tail. "That's quite a voice you have there, buddy," I said, giving him a pat on the head. In his eyes, rather than apprehension I thought I saw a hint of excitement.

I opened the door and my friend rushed in, along with a gust of cold winter air. I watched as the dog appraised our guest, fortunately with curiosity and little else.

"Hi!" she said. "So this is him? Wow, he is really big."

"Yup," I said. "He sure is."

"He's not going to attack me or anything, is he?"

"No, I don't think so." Nothing in the dog's behavior suggested aggression. "He's very gentle, and up to two minutes ago he's been very quiet."

She didn't look too convinced and was backed against the door. "That's quite a bark he has. I wasn't going to come in after I heard that."

"Yeah, that was interesting," I said. "I don't think you need to worry." I coaxed her out of the doorway and we sat down in the living room, with the dog hovering in his usual faraway corner.

She relaxed a little. "So, what's his name?"

"Well," I began, "he doesn't actually have one. At least, not a name that suits him or that he responds to." I told her the story behind the girl at the foster place calling him "Kong." "The name doesn't seem to suit him."

"No," she agreed. "He's big like King Kong, but he's not chained up or climbing the Empire State Building." By this point the dog had lain down in his corner and assumed his sphinx-like pose.

"That's exactly why I want to change his name. He needs one that suits his personality, not his size."

"How about Thunder?" she asked. "Fits the bark on him, I'd say."

"Not bad," I said, and looked over at the dog. "Hey. Thunder, do you like that name?" No reaction.

"Or what about Spot?" she suggested next. "That's kind of a cool, old-school dog name. And he does have that big black mark on his side."

"Spot! Here, Spot!" Again no reaction—just the laughter of my friend.

"I think he needs a human name," I said. "He has a lot of human features. He's like the kid in school who's so much bigger than all the other kids and is shy and quiet." The dog laid his massive head on the floor between his paws, completing the image.

"What about Oscar, like Oscar the Grouch on *Sesame Street?*" I wasn't sold. This was not a grouchy dog at all.

We stared at him for a few more minutes in silence, until a name occurred to me. "George," I said, and the dog immediately lifted his head and gave me his best Robert De Niro "You talkin' to me?" look.

"Did you see that?" my friend said. "He totally responded!"

"Is that you, George?" I asked. "Is that your name?"

Holding the look, he cocked his head and gave a slight wag of his big white tail—something I'd never seen him do. From that moment on, he was George.

EIGHT

The next day was a workday, which meant George's first day home alone. I was a bit apprehensive about leaving him, but I knew I had to try.

The morning walk, or should I say "morning drag," went fine.

That done, I grabbed my car keys to head out, but before I left, I got down on my knees to meet George at eye level. "Okay, George. So it's like this. I have to go to work to pay for that food you refuse to eat in front of me. I'll check in on you at lunchtime, but for now, you're in charge." George registered the keys in my hand and eyeballed me with his "I'm not going anywhere" look. When I made for the door, he did nothing, and when I was outside walking to my car, I stole a peek through the window. He remained exactly where he was, no spinning in circles with anxiety, no movement at all. I wasn't sure if I should be reassured or worried.

At the office things were fine, and for the first time in a while I had a bit of balance back. I had a great deal of affection and respect for the people I worked with. After Jane left, our CEO, Charlie Horsey, made a point of calling me regularly to check in and see how I was doing. I gave Charlie a quick call and got his voice mail: "Charlie, it's

Colin," I said. "Just letting you know that someone moved in with me this weekend. Pretty quiet, but hairy and drools a bit. Call me back." That would make him think. I walked over to Matt's office and gave him an update on George.

"That's amazing!" he said. "I'm so glad you got him."

Matt was as thrilled as I was and had lots of tips and advice. After catching up with him, I spent the rest of the morning returning emails that had accumulated over the weekend. In the back of my mind I was hoping George was okay and not nervously trashing the house. At noon I headed home to check in on him.

As I put the keys into the back-door lock, I heard a deep bark. I opened the door, and George was standing in the kitchen on high alert—head and ears up, chest out and nose twitching. As soon as he recognized me, he softened his stance slightly and sat down, but there was no coming to the door with his tail wagging—just a look that said, "Oh. It's you. Fine." On the plus side his food bowl was empty. "Hey, George. Did you have a good morning?" I asked, only to be eyed with suspicion. A quick tour around the house confirmed that everything was exactly as I'd left it—no "surprises" on the floor, nothing chewed up, no claw marks.

"Time for a quick trip to the yard," I said as I opened the back door. He stepped out cautiously and walked around a bit. It was an intensely sunny day, and his white fur stood out against the shadows cast by the fence. I was struck by how distinctive he was, and even with his challenges I liked him. "Okay. Time to go back in," I said after a few minutes. I might as well have been yodeling into the Grand Canyon. George retreated into a back corner by the garage and sat down facing me, as if to say, "No way." In a scene that would repeat itself in the weeks and months ahead, I slowly approached him and gently but firmly held on to his collar. It wasn't that he was being stubborn, not

exactly. It's that he would move only if I came with him, like he wanted me to escort him. I was starting to sense there might be more to George than met the eye.

I went back to work for the afternoon, and when I arrived home and put the keys in the door, I waited to hear that thunderous bark, but there was nothing. I opened the door to complete silence. "George?" I called out. More silence. He wasn't in the kitchen. I searched the dining room—nothing. "George, I'm home. Where are you?" The blue glow from the street shed a bit of light on the dog. He was sitting in the living room, staring straight ahead. I switched on the living room lamp, and now saw clearly that he was in the corner, alone, alert and upright, like an owl sitting on a fence. It was weird and almost eerie.

"Hey, buddy . . . What are you doing?" His eyes were so big and he didn't blink at all. It was as though he were afraid of the dark but didn't know how to get out of it. "Are you okay?" I asked as I knelt in front of him, putting my hand on the side of his big neck. Instantly he dropped his head, and for the first time ever stared down at the floor instead of at me. He looked beyond sad. He looked alone and terrified and hopeless. It was a look of total defeat.

I had watched teammates hold their heads the same way after losing important hockey games. I knew that look well, and I knew how it felt. I had let my head drop that way, most recently the night Jane left. It takes a tremendous amount of character to be gracious in defeat, to surrender to someone. I gently rubbed George's ears and brought my head closer to his. This has since become our thing, our secret way of communicating. "You're okay, George. You're safe with me. You're a good boy." He allowed me to whisper to him like that, face to face in a manner that was intensely personal, and even though he was sad, he was permitting me to move nearer. More than anything, I could see he was just tired of being afraid. After a few minutes I changed

my tone and brightly asked, "Do you want to go for a walk, big guy? You'll feel better after you have one of your giant pees." He slowly lifted his head and off we went.

Though technically the park across the street required dogs to be on leashes, a group of dog owners who regularly gathered there after work during the week let their dogs roam freely. As George and I started to cross the street from the house, he saw the dogs running and playing and he sat down in the middle of the street. "George, let's go." I gave the leash a tug and felt the "No way" ricochet up my arm. I was starting to figure out that sitting and watching was George's big move. It was actually a sensible strategy I was beginning to respect. The only problem was that he was sitting in the middle of the road. George had sidled up next to me, breaking the perfect equidistance he kept in the house.

"We can't stay here, big guy. We're going to get hit by a car. Let's at least make it to the sidewalk." Using all my strength, I "convinced" George over to the sidewalk, where he resumed his stubborn sit and continued to size up the people and dogs.

There were about a dozen dogs of various breeds, sizes and colors. There were also about a dozen people of various backgrounds, sizes and colors. Several formed groups, huddling together to stay warm. They all knew each other and clearly they knew each other's dogs, too. The young dogs were friendly and playfully wrestled, growling dramatically and posturing, tongues lolling. A few chased balls thrown or kicked by their owners, and the older dogs gingerly walked around sniffing and keeping their distance from the young pups. George was taking it all in.

Eventually a couple of young dogs broke free of the main group and wandered over to us. As they sniffed at George, who seemed indifferent to them, their owners followed after.

"Hey there. Nice dog. How long have you had him?" one man asked.

"This is day number three."

"He's so big!"

The man got closer and George shrank back immediately.

"Sorry," I said. "He's a bit wary of men still, even of me."

"No worries," the man said. Then he waved and went off to join another group of owners nearby.

A couple of women now approached. I happily explained that George was a Landseer Newfoundland and yes, his eyes were particularly droopy. And no, not all Newfs were black. And yes, he was a rescue. And no, he didn't bite. But yes, he was cautious. And no, he wasn't old, just over a year, even though he acted like an old man.

"So you're just a puppy," one woman said to George, rubbing his ears and crouching. George's giant tail slowly wagged behind him, and his eyes lit up in the dog equivalent of a goofy grin.

Another woman walked over and gave him a pat. "He's sure got a lot of fur," she said. I had no idea how to respond to that. A poodle mix appeared and gave George's rear end an aggressive sniff . . . and then just kept prodding, pushing and sniffing. "The poodle is mine," she added.

George's shoulders stiffened. "You know, I'm not sure he's used to being sniffed like that. Would you mind calling your dog away for a second?"

The woman turned to me as though I'd slapped her, and with a bit of anger in her voice said, "Looks like someone's dog needs training." Then she marched her poodle away.

Once she was gone, another woman nearby said, "Don't worry about her. Your dog's doing just fine."

I looked down at George, who had relaxed slightly after the poodle left. He softly bumped his shoulder into the woman who spoke, as if to say, "Pet me, please," which she did.

"You know, this is the most social I've seen him so far," I said. "He doesn't invite me to pet him like that."

"He's very sweet," she said. And at that, George's tail kicked up again.

"Have you thought about taking him to obedience school? It's actually not a bad idea, you know, so he can get used to you and to other dogs."

"Obedience school?" It had crossed my mind, but I certainly hadn't done any research into it yet.

"Yeah. It can really help a lot. And you might find that he learns to trust you more, too. Might be good for both of you—right, George?" she said, nuzzling his face. He closed his eyes and nuzzled her back. I couldn't believe this was the same dog that sat in my house like a statue, afraid to move.

The woman suggested Who's Walking Who, a school in the southeast end of the city. The irony of the school's name wasn't lost on me.

"Thanks, I think I'll give them a call," I said.

George and I returned home soon after, and I set about making dinner. I laid out his dinner bowl in the living room. "There you go, George. Eat up . . . when you're ready."

I went back to the kitchen table and started in on my own plate. But George lurked at the edge of the room.

"Come on. You have to be hungry," I said.

Nothing. Just that wide-eyed stare.

"All right then," I said. I ate a few bites of my food and opened my laptop. I Googled "Who's Walking Who." The school had great reviews. It offered a ten-week basic obedience course for dogs of all ages, shapes and sizes—which was great, considering George was an XXL. The next start date was two weeks away. I signed us up on the spot, and just as I did, I heard the crunch of kibble from the other room.

"You ready for school, George?" I asked. The crunching stopped.

As a kid I was never all that nervous about the first day of school, but when George and I arrived at Who's Walking Who for his—and my—first obedience class, I'll admit I had butterflies. The obedience class was held downtown in a high-ceilinged room that could have been mistaken for a dance studio if not for the rubberized floor. We arrived close to the start time, which didn't help my nerves, and the pure canine chaos that greeted us made George step back and try to tuck himself behind my knees.

The first thing I noticed was the sound assault, as the yapping of a dozen or more dogs ricocheted off the concrete walls. The fresh smells of dog breath had mingled with the permanent funk of puppy accidents to create a poignant aroma challenging for human nostrils. The place was a frothing sea of dogs sniffing, sprinting, panting, circling and wrestling their way around the room. There were pugs, bichons, toy poodles, Jack Russells and a solid contingent of mutts. I looked down at George, who was wide-eyed and leery. He was by far the biggest pupil in the room.

"You okay, George?" I asked as he cowered behind me, a response that could be read only as a definite no. "We can do this. We're in it together," I said, while I gently pulled him into the room.

As we made our way, there was a noticeable stir. People stared at the big kid moving to the front of the class. George kept his head down, sniffing the floor. He ignored a medium-sized doodle-something that came charging at him. We passed a tall, skinny guy and his black-and-white bulldog, and George gave them both a wide berth. I led him over to the instructors—a man and woman wearing Who's Walking Who T-shirts and sporting fanny packs full of dog treats. The woman was finishing registering an older lady with a terrified dachshund.

My grandfather Seymour Wylde Howes III, receiving a medal for bravery from General Bernard Montgomery for saving Allied soldiers from drowning at Juno Beach in World War II.

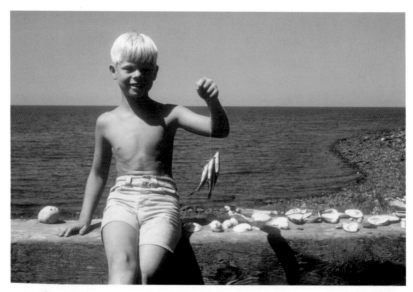

Here I am as a kid at my grandfather's cottage in Nova Scotia after doing one of the many "free days" activities we loved so much—fishing.

Visiting my beloved grandfather. He was 91 and I was 42. He passed away a few weeks after this photo was taken.

(*Left to right*) George, me and Todd on our way to California. By this point, George refused to remain in the back of the truck and commandeered the passenger seat, leaving me crammed in the tiny middle jump seat.

Still on our way to California, George enjoys running around in a field somewhere around Nevada. He's happy because he's finally got the front passenger seat.

George and me a few weeks after arriving in Los Angeles. Here we are on Hollywood Boulevard, star-gazing on the Walk of Fame.

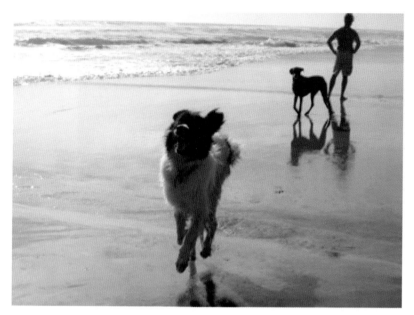

George running free for the first time at Huntington Beach in 2009.

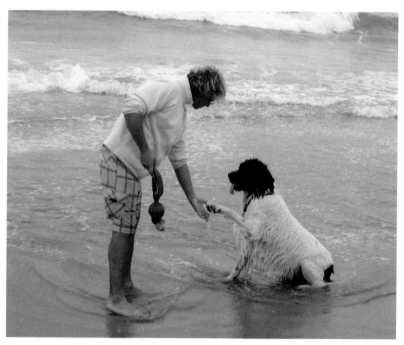

Playing ball with George—one of his favorite things to do.

A very young and goofy-looking George in 2009.

George has always had a soft spot for little dogs. At Huntington Beach in 2009.

George always looks extra cuddly after a bath. Here he is in L.A. in our full-sized SUV, which he makes look like a MINI.

George relaxing in our California home in 2009.

Hallowe'en in Los Angeles, 2009. George doesn't normally do the "dress up" thing, but he looked pretty funny for the the five seconds those devil horns stayed on his head. He was clearly not impressed.

George and I are picking up a rental surfboard for the very first time in 2009. I had no idea that I wasn't going to be riding solo.

Huntington Beach, 2009. George refused to let me surf on my own, so here we are going out on a board together for the very first time. George already looked like a pro.

George was comfortable on a surfboard right away.

Rinsing away the salt and sand at Bruce Jones's Surf Shop, Sunset Beach, 2009.

At the Surf City Surf Dog competition, the very first time George entered. He'd put on a great show in the first round, and here, as we awaited the finals, I kept wondering what was going on in that big head of his.

All warmed up, waiting for his heat.

The beach was packed, and George stood on his board, surrounded by competitors, awaiting the next round.

One of our "whisper moments" captured here just before the final round of the surfing championships in 2009.

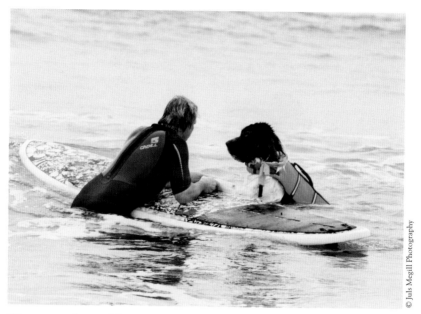

Waiting in the surf for our big wave. As he always does, George is looking me straight in the eye.

Getting George on the board in 2009.

There are not many pictures of George's first solo ride, but here he is discovering me in the water behind him.

George shaking off at the end of a long day of surfing.

Coming to shore after the finals in 2009. We had so much fun.

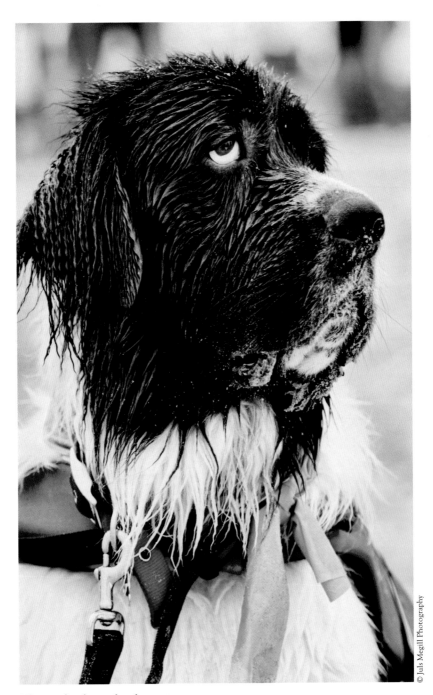

This is the face of a champion.

George found an especially appealing patch of floor and dropped to his belly to lick it.

"This must be George," the female instructor said when our turn arrived. "Aren't you a handsome boy!"

"Thanks," I said. George didn't look up, but at the sound of his name, his tail began thumping. The instructor bent to pat his head as George stayed focused on licking invisible delights off the floor.

"Stop licking and say hello," I said, giving him a quick tug on his leash. "Sorry about that."

She laughed. "Trust me, I'm used to it."

I launched into a long-form "history of George," even though I'd written all the info down previously when we registered. "He's a rescue, and he may have been abused, and he seems scared of men, and I'm worried that he doesn't take much interest in other dogs, and he kinda pulls a little—well, a lot—when I take him for walks, and—" I was rambling, and greatly relieved when the instructor cut me short.

"Don't worry," she said. "I read everything you wrote about him. He'll be just fine."

I looked down at the giant fur mound on the floor. He was still ignoring everything around him—the barking, the people, the dogs coming closer—and he was still stupidly focused on the rubber mat.

"Is this normal?" I asked.

"All part of the process. He'll get used to everything with time," she said. "You will, too."

Me? What was that supposed to mean?

"You can let him off his leash now. We'll start the class in a few minutes."

Let him off leash? Was she out of her mind? I'd never let George loose in a public place before, but who was I to argue with a professional? I unclipped him, half expecting—hoping—he wouldn't stray

too far from me. However, he immediately exercised his freedom and began exploring the room, while I wondered what to do with myself.

Observing him was revealing. He steered clear of all the men, but he wasn't shy with the ladies and boldly introduced himself to them all, approaching with his head lowered and his big tail waving like a fan. The women who weren't afraid of him gave him some pats and hugs, which he obviously enjoyed since he leaned his whole body weight against the women, causing a few gasps and peals of laughter. He also showed a sudden and passionate interest in the class's smallest dog, a teacup Australian terrier running figure eights through George's feet. George joyously bounced up and down on his front paws as the little dog tore circles around him.

Worried that he would accidentally step on the smaller dog, I yelled, "No! Careful, George!"

I was about to put the leash back on him, when the little dog bolted off to the other end of the room and George, unperturbed, moved on to a nearby fluffy, white bichon frise. The bichon probably weighed all of nine pounds to George's 140, but she wasn't scared at all.

I watched with trepidation, knowing that with one swipe of his paw, George might maim someone's beloved best friend, but again George surprised me. He lowered his massive head, his big tail wagging, and he gently touched the little dog's nose. He was as happy as a gorilla with a kitten, and he spent the next few minutes before class following the bichon around to the exclusion of everyone and everything else in the room, including me.

A few minutes later the instructors both turned to face the room. "If I could have everyone's attention," the male instructor shouted above the canine cacophony. "We're going to get started now, so if you could collect your dogs and form a line along the wall opposite the door—from smallest dog to largest—that would be great."

There were twelve dogs and twelve owners, and George and I were the biggest kids in class by far. The dachshund owner quickly found her shy, nervous dog and made her way to the opposite wall first.

"George!" I called out, but he was cavorting with the bichon and didn't even turn around.

The Jack Russell and a couple of Boston terriers dutifully followed their owners when summoned and found their rightful places in the line. The Frenchies, a lab and pugs, were easily corraled by their people and added to the line. The mutts did the same. George was still tailing the bichon, and as I made my way across the room to grab him, his new best friend was picked up easily by her owner and deposited in line beside the skinny guy with the black-and-white bulldog. With his new friend gone, George gazed up in confusion and then, totally spooked, ran away to a corner opposite the line.

"George!" I called out again—in vain. I didn't want to run to him and appear like a hapless owner who couldn't control his dog, so I sauntered over to him and said, "It's okay, George. Come." He summarily ignored me, arcing wide around me and then, like a queen greeting dignitaries, walked over to each pair in the lineup, tail wagging, and said hello.

"George! Come here. Now!" Nothing. I could feel the color spreading to my cheeks. I considered breaking into a jog, but I felt I might only make matters worse. As George continued licking hands and receiving pats on his big head, the whole line of humans started giggling. Finally the owner of the bichon took pity on me and hung on to George's collar long enough for me to catch up and take control.

"Thanks," I said as I dragged George to the big-kid end of the line.

"Okay," the male instructor said. "Looks like we're ready to begin . . . almost." He directed a small nod at George and me, and that was followed by a chortle from the group.

He and his co-instructor began the class by teaching the most basic of dog commands: "Sit." After showing us the correct way to address our dogs, complete with a hand signal to accompany the verbal command, we were asked to practice in a synchronized fashion. "Let's start with the wee one at this end and work our way down the line to . . . the big boy, George," the female instructor said.

From the bichon right on down to the Labrador beside us, every dog in line executed the move with ease—every dog, that is, except George. When it was his turn, I went through the proper motions, but he refused to comply. Not that he couldn't. George loved to sit and watch and look at things in his own good time. He just wouldn't do it when given the command.

"Sorry," I said, when the first try didn't work. "We'll give that another go. Sit, George. Sit. Si-i-i-i-i-i-it. George, SI-I-I-I-I-IT-T-T-T-T!"

Eventually, looking uneasy, he sat—for a second. Then his giant back end rose up and the giggles started anew. The other owners, it seemed, found this funny; I, however, found it far less so. The female instructor came over. "Try getting down to his level, and command him in a strong, authoritative voice," she said. She demonstrated, and of course George's rear end descended as obediently as though attached to a trained show dog. In my nine or ten tries afterward, he did the move a grand total of once. Just once.

"Good!" the instructor said in an overly bright voice. "You're doing great. Don't give up. Just be patient," she said, smiling at me and patting George for his "brilliant" performance. George wagged his tail happily and the second she walked away to help another dog, his caboose floated back up again to spite me.

The next command was "Down." The dogs would first sit, and then be led with a tap on the ground, a small tug on the leash and a gentle push on the shoulder. A treat and praise were given when the

dog successfully lay down on the floor. As the class started to practice, I heard enthusiastic and high-pitched calls of "Good girl!" or "Yes! You're so smart. Good boy!" The owners with the smaller dogs hardly had to do the shoulder press at all; they simply said, "Down," and their compliant little hounds prostrated themselves at their owners' feet.

For me it was like commanding a bag of wet cement. George was having none of it. And forget that new command "Down"; we were still having a whole lot of trouble getting the "Sit" part. Worse still, George wouldn't even look at me while I spoke to him.

Once again the female instructor came over. "Having a few problems?"

I absolutely hate being bad at things and, trust me, I am bad at a lot of things—yoga, singing, dancing, to name a few—so I've had a bit of experience with embarrassing public failures. But this was an all-new low. Clearly I was an awful dog handler, something made all the more obvious by having a dog weighing more than most of the other pupils combined, a dog bent on totally ignoring me.

The only thing I could think of doing to defend myself was to use some lame excuse: "He's probably having a hard time because he's so big, and, um, not really maneuverable, unlike some of the smaller dogs here." As soon as the words were out of my mouth, I felt even more stupid.

As I sheepishly eyed the floor, the instructor took the leash from my hand and gave a small tug to get George upright. George sprang to attention and stared into her eyes. "Sit," she said. Just once.

George dropped his rear to the floor, his head up and chest puffed out like he was just named "Best in Show."

The instructor smiled and, without missing a beat, swept her hand toward the floor and in a firm but gentle voice said, "Down."

Without hesitation George lowered his big body to the floor while maintaining eye contact with her. His execution of the command was perfect.

"Good boy, George. Good boy!" she said, as she dropped to one knee to rub his ears. George looked at her with eager eyes that asked, "What's next?"

"That was amazing," I said. "And embarrassing. Why won't he do that when I tell him?"

"Well . . ." she began, attempting to gather her thoughts. "First of all, he's a very smart dog, and I think he understands what we're trying to teach him."

"So, he's not 'slow' . . ."

"No, not at all—he's very bright," she said.

"So why won't he listen when I ask him to do things?"

"There's a lot going on behind those eyes, Colin," she said. "You can't take the refusal personally. Unfortunately defiance of the owner is common with dogs who've experienced neglect or abuse. It probably has nothing to do with you. And it's clear he prefers ladies to men."

Great, I thought. I have a gender-biased dog. A giant-sized, gender-biased dog, and I am the gender he's biased against. This isn't good.

"Is there anything I can do to fix this?"

"You're doing it. By bringing him here. That's the first step. He will figure out the rest eventually." At this point George rolled over on his back, exposing his belly.

"And one more thing," she said. "It's going to take time for him to trust you. Just try to be patient. Really patient."

"But—" I was about to ask her a whole bunch of questions about what to do and what not to do, if I was doing things right at home and if I was walking him right, what it meant when he did this or that, but George chose that moment to bound back up on all fours and barge into the practice of a cute little dog and its owner a few pairs away from us.

"I'll look after that for you," the instructor said, gently calling

George's name and handing me his leash when he came back to her right away and heeled at her side.

"He's going to need a lot of work, but I believe you've got a pretty special dog inside there," she said, before moving down the line.

I was not convinced. "Thanks," I said.

The rest of the class was a train wreck. George solidified his role as class clown, with me acting as his humiliated straight man. Any time I lifted my hand from his collar he'd find a dog that interested him and walk over, excited to say hello. At one point, perhaps sensing a potential learning opportunity, the male instructor stepped in to try to reason with him. George darted to the other side of the room. When the female instructor took over, George rolled onto his back and begged her for a belly rub. The sight of George's giant white stomach made her burst out laughing and whatever order she'd issued fell to the wayside as she petted him for what seemed like the hundredth time. My human counterparts in the room looked on with varying levels of amusement.

When class was finally over, I was defeated and exhausted. I suspected the instructors were, too, and as the female instructor said goodbye to George, I used the moment to issue an apology.

"I'm really sorry," I said. "It seems we're—I'm—not exactly good at this. Maybe it's best if we don't come next week. I don't want to distract the other dogs and owners."

"Nonsense," the instructor replied. "It was George's first class. He'll do better next week—won't you, George?" At this George did a perfect, solid sit. "See? He's a smart dog. He just needs some time to figure it out. You both do."

I hoped she was right. If I'd been the one with the tail, it would have been between my legs.

George and I spent the next week diligently practicing "Sit" and "Down." We did it every day, at least ten times during the morning

and evening walks. Sometimes he got it; other times he looked at me as if to say, "Why don't *you* sit?" Success was entirely random for seven days in a row, but random was better than nothing, and I was slightly encouraged.

We arrived for the next class early, and as we waited for the others to get there, I said, "Okay, George. You're going to be a good boy in class today, and I have to learn to trust you. Go have fun." Quietly fearing the same problems as last week, I let George off the leash to roam and socialize with the other dogs. George found his bichon friend and greeted her nose to nose, his three-foot-long tail wagging at a fraction of the speed of the bichon's mini wonder tail. A moment later, George flopped down and shoulder-rolled onto his back, at which point three or four other little dogs ran over and started sniffing him and licking him and tail-wagging all around him. The whole time, George's tail counted time in big thumps against the floor. A chorus of "Aw-w-w-w-ws" broke out, and suddenly the other dog owners were whisking out their cell phones to take pictures of the spectacle. Maybe he wasn't such a disruption after all.

George and I continued going to class for the next few weeks, and while I admit that I was starting to relax with time, I won't say that my palms were completely dry at the beginning of each class. I won't even say they were completely dry at the end of class. George was more of a sideshow than a pupil, and while he did learn a few things, it was unclear if that thing could really be called "obedience."

George still did a "hit and miss" sit, meaning he would do it one time out of every three or four attempts. The other dog owners in class

watched our tense standoffs, many of them muffling their chuckles or impatience. The female instructor would come to my rescue and help me, just to prove to me that George had it in him.

But George's biggest achievement occurred a few weeks later during our attempt to learn "off-leash recall." We were all standing along the wall, with the male instructor issuing his directives, when George sauntered out to the middle of the floor and had a big, slow poop in front of the entire class. Not his best performance.

At the end of that class the female instructor approached us. I thought for sure that this time she would ask us not to return, but she said, "I did some reading this week and discussed George's issues with some colleagues."

"You did?" I replied as I tried to keep—unsuccessfully—George in a heel.

"We think you need to stop relying on verbal commands and signals and start being more physical with him."

"Physical?" Did she want me to hit him? I was surprised and upset at her suggestion. "I won't do that," I said.

"No, no . . . I mean physical in a gentle way. I mean affection. You need to be affectionate with him."

She paused to let that sink in.

"Newfoundlands are a very sensitive breed. They read a great deal into tone of voice, even posture and body language. You have to work on that."

I got even more defensive. "But I'm so gentle with him and have been careful not to move suddenly around him. I rub his head and ears when he lets me."

"That's a good beginning," she said, "but you could afford to be even more affectionate with him." She paused again for a moment. "Do you hug him?"

"Well, no . . . not yet. He won't even eat in front of me, let alone let me hug him."

The instructor nodded slowly and looked down at George, who was standing still, staring at both of us. "He needs to feel love from you. He needs his faith in men restored." I stood there thinking about what she had just said to me, in a room full of people and dogs. "You need to make yourself more emotionally available. You need to learn to show love." Suddenly I felt very alone. It was almost the same advice Dr. Hamer had recently given me.

I felt my face getting flushed as I gazed at George's big, sweet face and sad eyes. I'd wanted to hug him since the minute I saw him and yet I'd always held back. Maybe I shouldn't have. But, to be totally honest, I'd struggled with giving physical affection all my life. I didn't exactly grow up in a family of huggers. In the past few months without Jane, this had only gotten worse. I wanted to help George. I really did. And I guess deep down, maybe I wanted him to help me, too.

I dropped to my knees in front of him and nudged his forehead with mine, taking his head in my hands. I could feel his warm breath against my cheek as I wrapped my arms around his neck and shoulders. Instead of recoiling, which is what I was certain he would do, he leaned into me and gently licked my face.

"There. You see?" said the instructor. "Was that so hard?"

I had to close my eyes to stop the tears from spilling out.

After a few more classes George started to show just how much he had going on behind those droopy eyes. I was now regularly getting down to his level to hug him and whisper in his ear. He would respond with soft licks, sometimes putting his big head on my shoulder. I noticed

that his confidence was improving alongside his desire to do things with me. Maybe this affection stuff was actually working.

Instead of being a regular disruption in class, George was slowly starting to pay attention and was learning the exercises. That didn't prevent an occasional "George moment" in which he would accidentally bump into one of the other handlers and send the person off balance when we were practicing an off-leash task. He knocked a few people down, but they were more startled than hurt. George always hung his head when he saw what he'd done, as though completely confused at how his "tiny" body could have caused such a result.

Beyond that, George was also figuring out his boundaries and even listening to instructional cues. Every time a trick was introduced or reviewed, the instructors would call a dog to the front of the class to demonstrate. They tried to mix things up so it wasn't the same dog every time, but the mix leaned heavily toward three or four smaller super-dogs—including George's girlfriend, the bichon frise.

She was a pro. Not only could she do all the basic commands, she could also balance on her hind legs when asked. Every so often, when owner and dog got bored with the normal drills, they'd practice elaborate tricks. I would have thrown them a few dollars if they'd put a hat out. Meanwhile, I was just happy when George managed to sit, lie down or come when I called him.

He continued to show modest improvement, and even though it was unlikely, I dreaded the thought that George might someday be called forward as the demo dog. That day did come, however; in week six, when the female instructor was preparing to demonstrate a sit-and-stay drill. She surveyed the class and said, "George, why don't you come up and show us how to do this one."

"Oh no," I muttered. I had George on his leash when she called him, and at the sound of his name he yanked me toward her, his

whole back end wagging. I held my ground . . . barely. The whole class laughed. "Are you sure you want George?" I asked, as I struggled to hold him back.

"Oh yes," she answered. "He can do this. Can't you, George?" He responded by dragging me the rest of the way across the room to where she stood. I handed her the leash. "He's all yours."

Sit-and-stay drills are as simple as they sound. The dog is asked to sit. When he obliges, he's told to stay, and then whoever's giving the commands slowly backs away while the dog stays put. A lot of dogs will get anxious as the owner backs away and they'll vent that anxiety by inching forward or just bolting off to their owner before being called.

George and I had practiced sit-and-stays many times. They sometimes worked, but more often things didn't go so well. Occasionally he'd sit for a while, but when I gave the command to come, he'd high-tail it in any direction except toward me.

But now, in the hands of the female instructor, he did the task to perfection, not only staying where he was supposed to but sitting regally, beautifully, with his head up and his eyes locked on her.

"Come!" she called after what seemed like an eternity. George pranced over to her and sat in front of her. When she gave him a treat, he turned and grinned at me like, "See? I got this."

I won't lie. It stung a bit that he behaved better for her than he did for me. I thought we were becoming a better team, but moments like this made me question it. At least he was pleased with himself—strutting around for the rest of the class with his chest puffed out like he owned the place. When she brought him back to me, she smiled and said, "He's doing so much better. He is definitely more open to taking direction. You're getting closer."

"Thanks," I said. "We're both trying hard." George sat with his head up and tail wagging.

Although I noticed that he was starting to follow me around in the house on his own, inside and outside class his recall with me still remained a problem. I was reading as many books as possible about dogs—Newfoundlands, in particular—and found out that not having razor-sharp recall wasn't completely unusual for Newfs. Many won't come when they're called, but they also don't want to be too far from their owners. Food in the form of cookies or other treats was recommended, but considering that George still wouldn't eat from his bowl in front of me, I was a bit skeptical.

While practicing in class, I'd tell George to sit and stay, and then I'd walk to the other side of the room and call him. If he came, I rewarded him with a treat, which he sometimes ate and sometimes didn't. Other more food-motivated dogs seemed to learn things at a faster rate. George learned what he was supposed to not from a desire for food but from watching his classmates and slowly, bit by bit, by paying attention to me.

A few weeks later he still wasn't the star, but he was catching on to the point of the class: that we were there to learn things together—and that he would get praise and hugs when, from time to time, he chose to listen. As he worked his way through various commands, he saw how happy it made me and how much love and affection I showered on him when he did as asked, and the praise alone started to work as motivation. Being a bit slow on the uptake became part of his charm, an element of the mountain of personality he'd hidden under all that apprehension. I was inwardly very proud of his improvement and couldn't help but love the gentle, sweet goofiness that was starting to define his personality.

On the final night of class we had our most memorable drill, and this time not because it was a disaster. The task involved gathering every person and dog in the center of the room, with owners and

leashed dogs randomly milling about in a cluster. On one side of that massive cluster of distraction, an instructor held the dog whose turn it was, while that dog's owner headed to the opposite side of the room and crouched behind a screen so the dog could only hear the owner but not see him or her when called.

Considering that even when George could see me perfectly, his reaction to being called was the dog equivalent of a shrug, I didn't think the odds of success were good for us. This was reinforced when the first few dogs, who normally zipped through new drills like they had been doing them all their lives, had trouble finding their owners. As George and I milled about in the center of the room, I could hear the pleas of the owners for their dogs to come, but the dogs often looked confused, and panicked before they eventually, sometimes several min-utes later, found their owners on the other side of the room. There was no way George would be good at this. He and I were in deep trouble.

When it was our turn, I took my place behind the screen and the instructor showed me where to peek out so I could watch George's reactions without being seen by him. He was on leash with the female instructor, on the opposite side of the room, and he was happily trying to nibble her neck and lick the side of her face. As instructed, I called his name with a sense of urgency in my voice. He immediately stopped licking, lifted his head and started scanning the room, looking for me. As the instructor let go of him, I expected him to go right back to licking her face, but instead he continued to vigilantly scan the room.

"George!" I called. "Come!" This time his head snapped toward the screen, and he intently made his way to my hiding spot. In fact, he was so intent that he didn't care who he knocked into or over on his way toward me. He was on a mission. I was shocked and amazed. When he got closer, I called again and he began to sprint. He flew around the screen and barreled into me. Tail wagging, he set about furiously

licking my face while I was lying on my back. He was so happy that he found me, but not as happy as I was.

"Good boy! You did great, George!" I said, as I wrapped him in a bear hug. He wagged and licked harder, and when released, he walked back to the instructor and the rest of the group with that same chest-puffed-out swagger he'd shown after doing the sit-and-stay drill. He found me quicker and with more intensity than any of the other dogs in the class that day had found their owners. I was so proud. All the frustration of the early classes fell away in that moment.

Later that night, when the final class was drawing to a close, awards for skills were handed out—such as "Best Sitter," "Most Consistent Stay," "Best on Leash." I was not expecting George would win any awards, and I was quietly making small talk with the owner of the bichon, who had just won an award for "Fastest Learner." George and the little dog lay side by side at our feet. Suddenly I heard "George!" followed by loud applause and even some cheering and scattered barks. George heard his name, too, and jumped to his feet and yanked me over to the beaming female instructor. She held an official-looking certificate in her hands, except that it had two cartoon dogs on the corners. At the top was the logo for the school and in the middle, written in big, red, felt-pen letters:

George
Most Improved Student

In the lower left corner was a hand-drawn heart. George dropped into a shoulder roll and showed his big belly to the room. "Good boy! You did great, George!" the instructor said as she rubbed his belly. He lapped up the praise and the applause from the rest of the group.

"And well done to you, too," she added, giving me a big smile.

"Thanks," I said, smiling back even harder.

Over the years I have been fortunate to win a few awards, both as an athlete and as a professional marketer. But of all the awards I have won—or co-won—I can honestly say that this handwritten certificate is the most satisfying award of all.

NINE

J ust like that, we were making progress. George and I were becoming a little closer, and we were both starting to trust each other—a little. Over the next few months our time together at home was characterized by two kinds of interactions: slow, deliberate movements and gentle, encouraging utterances.

I handled George with a degree of delicacy that probably was a bit too much, but in exchange he started to reveal his personality and unexpected quirks, beginning with the fact that he definitely had no clue just how big he really was. He knocked over chairs in the house, and would turn around and look at them as if to say, "Who did that?" He seemed completely unaware of the location of his own tail or shoulder—even his head. The tail, in particular, had many magical powers in the early days, with George blissfully oblivious of all of them. It could sweep, knock, smash, break and swipe almost anything placed on the coffee table. A glass vase, plastic water bottles (opened, of course) and the occasional half-consumed bottle of beer or glass of wine became acquainted with the floor, courtesy of George's enchanted tail. He even discreetly swept my keys off the table. I only found them unexpectedly, under the sofa, an hour after I needed them and had given up the search.

George also had a habit of wedging himself into spaces that would make the trunk of a smart car look expansive. He'd wedge himself between the coffee table and the couch, and then, immobilized, look at me as if to say, "How come I don't fit?" Occasionally he would venture under the dining table and get his body and legs caught in the jungle of chair legs and rungs. He would then issue one of his rare barks, which I'm fairly sure would translate into English as "Help me! I'm stuck under the table and I can't get out!" If I didn't come right away, he would start walking out on his own, dragging the chairs and the table with him.

In complete contrast to his size, he ate like a tiny, dainty dog, bit by bit, nibbling and then walking off for a while. "George, are you a ballerina in a Newfoundland's body?" No response.

Best of all, though, was the way he slept. Unlike most dogs, who usually circle and then carefully lower themselves to the floor, when George decided he wanted to lie down, he dropped and rolled his shoulder like a Hollywood stuntman. Once down, he would settle flat on his side for a few minutes and then perform the coup de grâce, pitching himself over onto his back with his legs splayed in all directions, belly aimed straight at the ceiling. "Very dignified, George. That's a noble pose." But the truth is it made me very happy to see him relax in front of me. He was no longer afraid that I would hurt him.

Once he'd stretched out for a while, his gangling limbs would find their way back under him and he'd curl up on the floor, taking up most of it, of course. Now it was time for a nap. When he was comfortable, he would drift off into the heavy sleep of giants and stay that way for hours. Then, once the epic snooze was over, he'd bounce back into being and give me a refreshed and surprised look that seemed to say, "I don't know what happened, but I sure feel rested. Let's go for a walk."

"Sure, George," I'd tell him. "It's park time." And we'd both

head to the front door, where I'd slip on his leash with ease while he wagged his tail to the tune of a rhythmic *bonking* as it hit the door or the wall or me.

At the dog park I'd even started to take him off leash. The first time had been a bit nerve-racking, because even though he'd done well at drills in obedience class, there was no way to really know what he'd do with his newfound freedom outside. I wasn't worried about him getting into it with other dogs, but I couldn't shake the fear that he could get startled by something and go running off, full tilt, into traffic on the busy cross street below the park. I built up to it, letting the other owners in the park know I was going to let him loose and asking them to keep an eye on him a good ten minutes before I finally took him by the collar and unclipped the leash.

For the first few seconds he just stood there looking up at me: "What now?" Then he dropped his nose to the ground and started sniffing. Though he wasn't driven by his stomach like other dogs, George was like a beagle when it came to smells, basking in them more than most dogs do. Nose down, he ran over to a bunch of bushes and began inhaling them. Then he moved on to a tree and then another, some more bushes, a piece of playground equipment and back to the trees, breathing everything in like the Big Bad Wolf in reverse. A few other dogs approached him at various points, sniffing at his face and his rear and then bouncing into the bowing pose dogs use to say, "Let's play." George seemed confused by the body language and uninterested in his fellow canines. He eyed each potential playmate quizzically for a second and then got back to his sniffing.

I gave him roughly five minutes on his own before calling him back. He returned to the first clump of bushes and buried his nose in them for a while and then started walking farther from me. When he was about thirty yards away, I got a little anxious and I started to walk

toward him. He glanced back at me but continued on his merry way. He didn't run, and it didn't seem like he was trying to escape; he was just being defiant, as though he was saying, "Look, I've got more sniffing to do here, so lay off, man."

"Okay," I said. "Don't go too far." I let him get a bit farther, but when he showed no sign of stopping, I picked up my speed. "George!" He still didn't come to me, but this time he stopped and waited. I closed the rest of the gap between us as he gazed up at me with a big question mark in his eyes. "You can't go wandering off on me, George," I softly scolded. "I get worried about you." He leaned into me and licked my left hand. I took his collar with my right. "Come on, let's go," I said. I led him back to the spot where the other dogs were playing. He didn't resist and stuck by me until it was time to go home.

The next few days were somewhat better, and George was able to come when called—eventually. It usually took him a few repeats, but I was feeling good that he actually listened, and the visions of my beautiful, big Newf running out into traffic began to fade from my mind. The dog park became a place we both were excited to visit. George enjoyed the sniffing and meeting new dogs, and I had a chance to socialize with people in my neighborhood. Small talk about dogs or the weather was actually helpful in getting me back on track socially. With the focus in our community on four-legged companions, no one asked me about Jane. The outing was low stress, and it was slowly starting to become comfortable. As well, our daily walks had begun to replace my solo stints outside on the back porch with a drink and multiple cigarettes. I was beginning to feel a bit better about myself. And it was hard to have a bad day when at the end of it all, George was wagging his tail at the front door, ready to lick my face and wash my anxiety away.

At night when I was ready to crash, he'd jump down and take up his usual spot on the floor, near my bed. No matter how uncomfortable

he got, though, he never once used his expensive dog bed. It continued to collect dust on the floor like a museum piece.

Our only setback came a week or two after I first started letting George off his leash at the park. There was a man who frequented the park to walk his dogs but who never talked to anyone or even approached the main group. He was of medium height, and he wore tinted, thin-framed glasses, but apart from the glasses he was among the most nondescript people I've ever seen. His one distinguishing feature was the pair of snow-white Pyrenees, both nearly George's size, that he walked side by side, never letting them off their leashes.

This was maybe the fourth time I'd seen him in my two and a half months of twice-daily park visits. He entered the park from the street I lived on and cut into a soccer field about forty yards away from where I was standing and talking with a handful of other owners. George was already in the field, exploring by himself, and as the man made his way across it, George took an interest in the dogs and strolled over to them. Trusting George more now, I stayed put as he went to say hello. George was about ten feet away, when one of the Pyrenees made a run at him. It reached the end of its leash in short order and stopped, snarling, baring its teeth and straining to get at George as the man held it back. The second dog stood back, staring at the commotion.

George had shown himself to be only a sweet, shy and gentle soul, despite his size and strength. He'd displayed no aggression at all in obedience school or when off leash at the dog park. Whenever he encountered an aggressive dog, even one a fraction of his size, George would always back away, leaving the other dog without a

target. He never stood up for himself and never barked when confronted. Except this time.

George thundered a deep bark back at the Pyrenees. When I heard him, I began running toward him and the man, who was yanking on the leash to maneuver his one angry dog away from George and back beside its calmer partner. I'd taken no more than five steps, when I heard the man yell something at George that sounded like "Go away!" Then he ran at George and aimed a violent kick at his head.

George saw the blow coming and managed to duck it, the boot missing him by inches. I was still thirty yards away, so I broke into a run, yelling, "What the hell are you doing?" George had turned and bolted, wide-eyed, toward me, but not before the guy tried to take another kick at him.

"Get your dog on a leash!" the man yelled as I got closer. "This isn't a leash-free park." His two dogs were now growling and baring their teeth as I approached. George, meanwhile, ran right by me and stood ten yards behind, terrified.

"Are you out of your mind?" I said. "Your dogs are being aggressive, and you're going to kick my dog for barking back?"

"My dog's on a leash. He can do whatever he wants," he yelled. "Your dog's off leash! I'm going to get you fined!"

Not that having spent a year in therapy makes me an expert, but I would be wholly willing to testify that this guy was nuts. I turned around to make sure George was okay. He was still standing a ways off, watching the scene. "Do whatever you want," I called over my shoulder in disgust as I headed to George.

When I reached him, his head was down and his tail between his legs. He was shaking all over. The guy and his two big dogs started walking toward us and kept yelling, but I ignored him, bending to talk to George, instead. "You're okay," I told him, rubbing his head.

"Everything's okay." George leaned closer, as though he wanted to hide underneath me. I tried to soothe him, but the shaking didn't stop. I clipped his leash back on.

"I'm going to call the police!" I heard. I felt the anger bubbling up inside me.

"Yeah? You tried to hurt my dog. It's a minor miracle I haven't beaten the crap out of you."

My threat wasn't serious—though I would've loved to see it through—but it had the desired effect. The man finally turned around with his dogs and fled the park. George had lain down behind me and buried his head between his paws, still trembling. I sat down on the ground beside him and bent over to hug him.

"It's okay, big guy. No one's going to hurt you. Never again, George. I won't let that happen." I felt a big head nuzzle my chest, trying hard to disappear under me. Everyone else in the park had seen at least a chunk of the encounter, and as I sat with George burying himself into me, a group of people walked over.

"Is George okay?" one of them asked.

"Yeah, I think so. The kicks didn't connect, but they came close. I think he's just really scared."

"That guy's crazy," someone else said. "He's done stuff like that before." I didn't find this particularly comforting.

I gave George some time to collect himself and then coaxed him up and took him for a slow walk around the park. Other owners arrived to check on him and lend some words of comfort and support, and many of their dogs seemed to do the same, which was nice, but George was rattled. He kept looking behind him and was no longer interested in sniffing, or in meeting new dog friends. I walked him back home, and when we got there, he crawled into a corner of the living room and lay down on the floor.

When it was his dinnertime, I brought his food bowl over. "Here you go, George." He turned his big droopy eyes to look at me, and when I put the bowl down, he sighed and turned away.

He didn't eat that night. No crunching at all, even when I was out of the room. And the next morning, when I grabbed his leash to tell him it was time for his walk, he trailed behind me on our way to the door.

"What's up, big guy? Don't want to go to the park today?" No eye contact at all.

"We've got to get back out there, George. If we don't, the bullies win. Come on," I said, giving him a good pat and clicking his leash on.

I decided to take him around the neighborhood instead of straight to the park, and he seemed quite pleased that we weren't headed in the usual direction. We didn't run into any familiar faces—welcome or otherwise—George did his business, and when we got back home, I heard him crunch away at some kibble before I went to work.

That night I knew we'd have to face the park again. I let him get acclimatized for a long time before freeing him from his leash. When I finally did, he stuck close by me and literally just stood around. He didn't sniff or play with the other dogs, and when I clipped his leash back on, he actually seemed relieved.

It took George a couple of days to get back to acting like himself. All the progress we'd made since he'd arrived at my house seemed lost— he barely ate, hid in corners around the house and was noticeably anxious. There was one important distinction, though: he didn't shrink from me. In fact, quite the opposite. He lay beside me on the couch at night while I worked or watched TV; he climbed into bed with me and slept right beside me. Out in the world, he stayed glued to my side in the kind of perfect "heel" position I'd always wanted him to adopt in obedience class. Maybe in the light of some crazy person who wanted to kick him,

I suddenly didn't look so bad. Or maybe he was just happy I'd stuck up for him. Either way, after a few days of walking on eggshells, he found a way to let me know when he was finally feeling better.

I was in the living room watching TV and heard a growling from the second floor of the house. George never growled, so I was kind of confused, and then my confusion turned to concern. I climbed to the second floor and popped my head into the bathroom at the top of the stairs, which was roughly where I thought I'd heard the sound coming from. The toilet and shower and deep soaker tub were all right where I'd left them, but George was nowhere to be found.

I headed to the guest bedroom and then I heard it again—a rumbling loud enough to shake the house on its foundation and most definitely emerging from the bathroom. I walked back into the bathroom, and this time I went right in. I looked over the edge of the tub, and there was George, fast asleep, flat on his back, his gangly legs akimbo. His huge head was angled to one side, and his big, open mouth and wet nose were pushed up against the tub wall.

He took in a big breath, and when he let it back out, he snored right against the side of the tub. The whole thing vibrated, amplifying the noise, and there it was—that deep foghorn blast I'd heard from downstairs.

I laughed so hard I woke George up—how his own snoring hadn't, I'll never know. He leaped from the bath, tail wagging, and looked up at me curiously, as if to say, "What did I miss? What's so funny?"

I bent down and gave him a giant hug. "Feeling better . . . Sneorge?" I said. When I heard the *thump, thump, thump* of his happy tail against the floor tiles, I knew the answer was a resounding yes.

TEN

Living with George brought some balance to my life, balance that I hadn't had in a long time. I actually had a reason to leave work every night and something positive to focus my energy on when I got home. And George continued to improve. We were much more relaxed around each other, and I could tell he was happy to see me when I walked through the door at the end of the day. I sure was happy to see him, too.

But that didn't stop me from working hard during the day. I loved my job, and I still needed a distraction from thoughts about Jane, most of them not very helpful. In the spring of 2009 as I flew down to New York for my annual job review, the economy was on shaky ground and most days there were articles in the newspapers of sizable corporate layoffs. Even though I had developed several large projects and had good relationships with clients and co-workers, I was a bit concerned about my upcoming review. One thing was certain: I did not bring any of my personal problems to work. In fact, to distract myself, I worked twice as hard after Jane left. Still, in a difficult economic environment anything is possible, and it was hard not to be anxious as I packed my suitcase, with my big dog watching my every move.

This was going to be my first time away from George and that was concerning, as well. I dropped him off at a highly recommended kennel. It was only for one night, I kept telling myself. He would be fine. As I registered him at the front desk, he leaned against me and I could feel him shaking. I knelt and took his head in my hands. "It's going to be okay," I said. "I'll be back before you know it." His eyes drilled into mine with a panicked look that broke my heart. How could I do this to him?

A male kennel worker took the leash from me and said, "Okay, George. Come with me. We're going to have a great time together." That's when George dropped to the ground and gave us the now-familiar "I'm not going to move" look.

"He's kind of afraid of men," I said. The guy eyed me like I was a bit nuts. As he was re-evaluating George's determined look and his bulky frame glued to the floor, the receptionist had an idea.

"Go get Jennifer," she said.

Jennifer arrived and soothed George with lots of cooing, and George followed her—albeit reluctantly—to his temporary home.

"Bye, George," I said. He turned his head my way for a last glimpse before leaving the room. How could I explain to him that I wasn't leaving forever? I couldn't.

"I'll see you tomorrow," I said. And off I went to the airport.

I arrived several hours later at MKTG's headquarters situated in Chelsea Market, a hip and historic district on the edge of the Hudson River in southwest Manhattan. I spent much of the morning catching up with friends and touching base on a few projects and then, just before lunch, knocked on Charlie Horsey's door.

Charlie was my boss and MKTG's CEO. He is easily one of the most savvy minds in American advertising; however, at first glance he looks like the guy next door: tall, clean-cut, casually dressed in a dark

sport coat, jeans and a buttoned-down shirt. He was wearing some very colorful Nike kicks on his feet, though. Charlie was the kind of boss who could sit in on a brainstorming session, hear strategies people had been developing for weeks, even months, and then suggest a better one off the top of his head, all the while managing not to offend anyone. He was tough but fair, and crazy smart.

"Colin, it's great to see you! Come on in," he said as he gave me a handshake and a hug and waved me into his office. I asked about his wife and four kids; he knew Jane was gone and did me the favor of not dwelling on it much. Instead I told him all about George.

"So a dog, huh?" he said.

"Yup. It's great having him around. He's been really good company."

We talked about a few other things, and when we were good and caught up on our personal lives and a few business issues, he opened a folder on his desk.

"So," he said with a great big grin. "Ready to be reviewed?"

"As I'll ever be."

"I want to start by saying that I'm well aware of the challenges of pitching new business in Canada—especially in this type of year—and we've been really happy with the relationships you've built."

He paused. "You're waiting for the 'but'?"

I nodded.

"Well, the 'but' is that the progress you've made hasn't been quite what we were hoping for."

He was right. Everybody was struggling and my office was no exception. "Charlie, I realize things could be better, but—"

Before I could finish my sentence, Charlie interrupted. "We've just completed a deal to buy an agency in Los Angeles," he said. "We think there's a lot more promise in that market than we're finding in Canada right now."

My heart sank. The worst-case scenario was about to happen. He was going to close the Toronto office—I was going to lose my job.

Charlie studied my face for a moment. "This new office in L.A. will bring us some exciting opportunities. We need someone to run the place, lead our culture and the way we do business. I've decided that person should be you."

I was sure I'd misheard, misunderstood, mis-something-ed. "Sorry?"

"Colin, we're transferring you to Los Angeles."

"Los Angeles, California?"

"No, the other Los Angeles, the one in Wisconsin," he said, laughing. "Of course California."

"I'm moving to L.A.?"

"You've got the experience, you're great with clients and employees, and we need someone senior on the ground out there who can help us navigate this merger." He leaned over and lowered his voice. "It will be great for you personally, and it's the right time in your life to have a fresh start like this."

He let that sink in and then continued. "Plus I know you're a hockey player, but you look like a surfer. You'll totally fit in."

The whole conversation was surreal, like it was happening to someone else. "So, I'm going to L.A."

"Yes!" He reached out to shake my hand. "We will have your work visa all sorted out. We want you there as soon as possible. Welcome to America, my friend! Are you in?"

As a kid growing up in a small town, I never imagined that someday I would be sitting in a fancy office in New York City about to accept a job as an executive in Los Angeles, California. I thought of my grandfather. I thought of our walks on the beach and how he always taught my brother and me that hard work pays off and that taking on new challenges is a good thing. I wished I could have called him then, just to hear his voice.

I think he would have been proud. I also knew that Charlie was right about the fresh start.

I smiled and looked up at Charlie. "Okay. I'm in," I said as I reached out and shook his hand.

"Great! You'll start in six weeks. We've got a town house lined up for you in Hermosa Beach. Paul will help you with the visa and the financial stuff. Any other questions?"

"Just one," I said.

"Is the town house big enough for a 140-pound dog?"

ELEVEN

After an evening dinner and small celebration with Charlie and other MKTG friends, I grabbed a flight home the next morning and headed to the kennel to pick up George. It was starting to sink in that I had agreed to move to the U.S., to Los Angeles, a city I had only seen in the movies.

I thought about George on the flight back. How would he take to moving yet again? And what about the weather? Would it be too warm for him? Things were starting to fall into place with us, and we now had a routine that included walks, eating, sleeping and as many hugs as I could give him each day. Dogs like structure and I suspected George liked it even more than most dogs. And here I was, about to move him across the continent to a new home, a new city, a new country, even a new climate.

I pulled into the kennel with all these thoughts on my mind, plus one more: I missed him and couldn't wait to see him. I wondered, had he missed me?

"We'll bring him right out," the receptionist said. "He was a very good boy."

As soon as George laid eyes on me, he went crazy with excitement. "George!" I said, kneeling on the ground, and he rushed to

me and nearly knocked me over. "It's so good to see you," I said, burying my head in his neck as he licked my face. He was wagging his tail so hard his entire back end shook from side to side, and when I got to my feet, he jumped up and put his big paws on my shoulders in a bear hug. He looked me in the eye and then started licking my face. He nearly knocked me back to the ground. All I could do was laugh.

"I missed you, too, big guy!"

The kennel employees watched as the big dog continued his excited dance, bouncing on the floor and spinning in a tight circle. I thanked the staff and gave George a gentle tug on his leash. "Let's go, buddy," I said. "Let's go home. I have some big news to tell you."

Navigating the city traffic on the way home, I told him out loud about the meeting in New York. Yes, that's right: I talked to my dog. He cocked his head and listened with rapt attention. "George, we're moving to Los Angeles." I told him all the details about the new job, what was good about it and what I was concerned about. I told him about my work visa and the timing and that we'd have a new home by the beach. Now, I'm not so crazy as to think that George understood what I was saying, but there's no doubt that he was an excellent listener, and it helped me to articulate everything.

"Here we are, George," I said as we pulled into the driveway. I opened the door and George trotted right in the house—our house. Within a few minutes we were back to our very comfortable domestic routine, no worse for wear from our first night apart.

The month and a half between being offered the job transfer and the day George and I actually left Toronto was a total blur. At work I was

tying up loose ends and getting familiar with the Los Angeles client case studies. At home I was deciding what to bring with me and how to get it to California, as well as learning how to take a dog across the border.

I also had to think more deeply about what to do with the house—a house that Jane and I still co-owned. I decided it was best to sell it, but that meant I'd have to contact Jane. We'd been split up for more than a year by that point and had barely spoken since the end of couples' therapy. Every once in a while I'd experience something profound and have the urge to share it with her. Especially after I got George, I'd wanted to call her and say, "Guess what? I got a Newfoundland dog, and he's great!" But ultimately I stopped myself, because the person I so desperately wanted to connect with didn't exist anymore—at least, not for me—and I knew that by reaching out, I'd be left feeling lonelier than before I'd called.

This time was different, though. This time I was calling Jane out of practical necessity. Not knowing her new home number, I phoned her at work. I'd been prepared to leave a voice mail, but she picked up on my first attempt.

"Jane speaking." It was the same voice I recognized and loved, but it sounded odd to hear it after all this time.

"Hi, it's me," I said. "How are you?"

"What's up?" she asked. I couldn't hear any emotion in her voice.

I moved right to practicalities. "I've got a new job. I've been promoted and am moving to Los Angeles. I think we need to sell the house."

"Oh," she said. "Okay."

We figured out the details quickly and easily. "That works for you?"

"It does," she answered.

"Well, I guess that's it then." I paused. I wanted so much for her to ask me how I was, what else was new—anything. It was a foolish hope.

"Okay, well . . . that's really it. Bye, Jane." I hung up without waiting for her to say goodbye in return.

When I put down the phone, George was lying beside me on the couch, his back end closest to me. With great determination, he turned his big body around so he could lay his head in my lap.

"You're a good boy, George," I said. And instead of falling apart, as I thought I would after a conversation like that with Jane, I rubbed his big, velvety ears and felt . . . okay. I was still anxious, I was still hurt and I was definitely sad, but I wasn't broken. And I wasn't going under, not this time.

As I sat there, I remembered when my grandfather first taught me to swim. I couldn't have been more than a couple of years old. He took me by the hand and walked me out into the ocean. "It's not that cold," he said with a wink, knowing full well it was. And when the water got too high, he let me wrap my arms around his neck so that I'd learn to float in his wake. As an adult, it wasn't lost on me that this is exactly how he'd earned a medal for bravery in World War II. Injured Allied troops drowning on Juno Beach wrapped their arms around his neck and he swam them through machine-gun fire to the safety of shore. He did this several times, until he was ordered to stop and seek safety inland.

"You're okay, my boy," he'd say to me as I clung to his neck, but I was never scared, because I was with him. When I was older, he taught me how to hold my breath underwater.

"Remember—always keep your eyes open."

"But, Grandpa, it stings."

"It only hurts for a second. Then you get used to it."

Because I knew he was telling the truth, because I trusted him,

I tried it. And he was right. It was uncomfortable, but not for long. Soon enough the sting went away, and a whole new underwater world opened up before my eyes.

As my big move to L.A. approached, I needed to let Dr. Hamer know that I was relocating, and to get a bit of perspective on things. I wanted to find out if I would be okay, if I was really ready for such a big life change. I wasn't sure that I was. I still worried that George might not be ready for another move. Both things had me preoccupied. It had been almost fourteen months since I started seeing Dr. Hamer, and I was very hopeful that he would say I was ready to go.

Lying back on the couch, I revealed my big news about moving and my brief call with Jane.

"I can recommend a new doctor in L.A., if you'd like."

"Seeing someone there would be costly. My health insurance won't cover it in the States," I said. "Besides, I think I've gotten better."

Silence.

"I've progressed, haven't I? Maybe not a hundred percent, but I definitely feel better."

"Do you want me to tell you that you're fine?"

"Well, yes . . . but not if it isn't true."

"Why do you feel you need me to tell you you've gotten better?"

"It's been over a year. I've been trying really hard. I'd like to know what you think."

He didn't look up from his pad but smiled. "You've definitely made progress and aren't as wobbly as you were early in our sessions, but you're also right that you're still not a hundred percent."

"Okay. That's fair," I said.

"I think there have been signs of improvement, but it's important that you recognize them rather than have me tell you them." He waited a minute to let that sink in. "Let me change the subject. Do you think you have helped the dog you adopted?"

I lay there on the couch through an awkward silence and gathered my thoughts. "You know, the crazy thing is that I rescued this dog, but there are some days when I wonder if I've got it backward."

Dr. Hamer nodded and scribbled away on his pad. "What do you mean by that?"

"I don't really know," I said, and meant it. "We finished obedience training a couple months ago. George was really bad at the beginning. Couldn't follow a single instruction. He was a mess."

Dr. Hamer chortled.

"One of the instructors at the school gave me some good advice on how to help him, and so I did it."

"Did what?" Dr. Hamer's pen was poised.

"I hugged him," I said. Tears welled in my eyes as I lay there looking at Dr. Hamer's ceiling. I knew every crack and small stain on it.

"The instructor said that George might start to be a normal, happy dog if he could leave his past behind. And she told me to hug him."

"So do you think you have to do the same thing as George? Do you have to leave your past behind?"

I hated when he did this—turned the discussion back to me, when all I wanted was to talk about something else.

"I guess so. Yeah," I said.

"Do you think it would help if someone hugged you? Does George hug you?" he asked.

Since I had not grown up in a demonstrative family, the one thing I had loved about Jane was that she was not shy about holding my hand or giving hugs.

I struggled to answer. I thought about how George leaned all his weight into me whenever he said hello, and how the moment I picked him up at the kennel after being away a day, George jumped up and put his big paws around my neck.

"Yeah," I said. "I guess he does hug me."

"Well, it sounds like you are off to a good start."

California Dreaming

TWELVE

There's a reason most dogs you see on TV shows and movies set in California are short haired and small. It's hot there. Really hot. And as the weeks passed and our date for going to California approached, matters got worse when wild fires erupted throughout Los Angeles County, heating things up even more. I started to worry more about George and how he might react to the heat. I worried that this move might be the worst possible thing—physically and emotionally—I could do to him right now.

I decided to call the Hermosa Beach Animal Hospital and talk directly to someone who knew how the weather might affect a large, furry dog like George. A very cheery receptionist greeted me on the phone. When I told her where I was calling from, she said, "Lots of snow there today?" It was mid May and seventy-one degrees Fahrenheit in Toronto. Obviously this woman didn't know much about Canadian weather.

I changed the subject. "So, I'm just wondering if Hermosa Beach is safe for a big, furry dog, especially with the wild fires blazing. I'm moving there with a Newfoundland and I'm curious about whether it will be cool enough for him," I said.

Silence. It was the Canadian equivalent of asking her if she lived in an igloo. After a long pause, she said, "I think you're pretty safe from the wild fires because we're right on the ocean. They generally burn pretty far away from here. And the temperature by the beach rarely gets higher than seventy-two degrees—perfect for humans and dogs alike." I could almost hear her rolling her eyes.

"Okay," I said, sheepishly. "That's good to hear. I think he can manage that."

"Great," she said. "So maybe we'll see you and your Newf at our clinic someday, provided the wild fires don't get you first." Despite my embarrassment, I pretended to laugh along. I took down the clinic's information for future reference and hung up the phone with one less thing to worry about.

Next thing I investigated was how I would get George, myself and all our belongings down to L.A. I decided to drive. A road trip: a man and his dog. What could be better and more basic than that? I'd rent an air-conditioned truck, and George would be only a look-in-the-rear-view away from me. That meant we'd be able to stop along the way as often as George needed to take care of business and to sniff to his heart's content. It would be a great American adventure!

Then I calculated the driving hours and realized my solo driving mission might be more difficult than I thought. It was going to take a good five or six days. I needed a wingman, so I called my best friend, Todd. I had really opened up to Todd and his wife, Sheila, in those first rough months after Jane left. We had originally been teammates on a hockey team and had often stuck up for each other in the odd scrap or two. We had remained close friends for over twenty years. He was one of the people I knew I would miss most when I left. There weren't many interests we didn't share—hockey, golf, comedy shows and the occasional beer being the biggest—but

there was one huge difference in our shared interests: Todd didn't like dogs.

On a Thursday morning we were playing golf and Todd was attempting a difficult uphill putt over a slight ridge in the green. I was filling him in on my plans. "I'm going to drive to L.A.," I told him. "I've already got a small moving truck booked."

"That's a hell of a long drive." He hit his ball firmly, reading the break perfectly so the ball veered to the left in the last two feet and into the hole. "I'm in!"

"Nice putt. You're in? In for the hole or in for the drive?"

"Both," he said with a big grin. "I think the drive will be fun!"

"It's going to take more than a few days."

"Just don't make me share a seat with that dog. Besides, you drive like an old lady and I don't want you getting lost on some interstate in Iowa. Someone's gotta look out for you."

The road trip would give Todd and me a final few days to hang out and yet another thing to laugh about. I was going to miss him, but he was right—the drive would be fun.

I got the truck first thing on a Monday morning and Todd arrived not long after I'd parked it in front of the house. We had intended to hit the road by ten that morning, but as with every road trip in recorded human history, we didn't get out the door until hours later.

Todd was a lifesaver when it came to loading the truck. Six-foot-three and weighing about 240 pounds, he could carry way more than most people. He was big like George, but as he'd said, he sure wasn't a dog person. I had tried to explain about George's personality and issues, but Todd was indifferent. "Hey, I respect that you're helping that big

dog out, but you deal with him. I just want to get this truck loaded and on the road." George, already known for his fear of men, actively avoided Todd, shying from him every time he walked by. George whined as we packed away the contents of the only safe home he'd ever known. Meanwhile, I was feeling surprisingly good. Although I had a great house and I had worked hard on renovating it, the place still had Jane's imprint all over it. I needed and wanted to leave it behind. Today that was going to happen.

Once we were all loaded up, it was time to go. The cab of the truck had two captain's chairs and a tiny, low jump seat between them. It was pretty clear that George wouldn't fit up there with us, so we set George's travel crate up in the back of the vehicle. The crate was huge, designed for airline travel and big enough for him to curl up in and sleep.

"C'mon, big guy, jump in," I said. George wasn't overly impressed. He looked worried and sad and sat like a stone statue, staring straight through me. It reminded me of that scene in the movie *Rain Man* when Tom Cruise is trying to get his autistic brother, played by Dustin Hoffman, into the car for a cross-country drive but he will have none of it. It was funny, but it also wasn't funny.

I got down on my knees and whispered into George's soft, velvety ear. "It's okay, George. We are moving to a new home. Just you and me. And it's close to the ocean. You'll get a chance to swim, which is what you and all your relatives are meant to do."

He leaned into me as I held out his favorite toy, the giant stuffed donut I'd bought him the first day I had him. It was in tatters despite being advertised as "rip-proof." I placed the shredded toy in his crate. "Get your donut, George! Let's go." George jumped into his crate. I closed the thick wire-mesh door and said, "Good boy. We'll stop in a couple of hours for a break." I closed the back of the truck, said goodbye

to the house, locked the front door, looked at the For Sale sign in the front yard and pulled away from the curb—no photos, no tears and no looking back.

Todd and I shared the first stint of driving equally that day, making it to the border at Detroit by ten that night after a few pit stops for George along the way. Every time we let him out, there was an ordeal of pleading and coaxing to get George back into his crate. Todd clearly wasn't growing any fonder of this dog.

The wait to get across the border wasn't too bad, given that it was late on a Monday night. Our turn came and I nervously pulled up to a booth. Crossing the U.S.–Canada border in either direction is not an exact science. I had done it dozens of times, but this was different. MKTG had filed all the paperwork on my behalf and had lawyers coach me on what to say during the customs interview, which I was told could last anywhere from thirty to sixty minutes. I hoped I'd get a customs officer who was casual and friendly, asked minimal questions and would wave us through quickly. I had vet papers for George, assuring his good health, but still, I worried that something could go wrong.

"Passports," the customs officer said. I handed them to him. "Which one of you is Colin?"

"That would be me."

"Where are you fellows headed?"

"Hermosa Beach, California."

He looked surprised. "That's a long ways away. How long are you planning on staying?"

"Years, I hope. I'm starting a new job there. I've got my L1A visa here for you to process." I held up my mound of papers.

"You working down there, too?" the officer asked Todd.

"I'm just along for the ride. I'll be coming back."

"Okay," the officer said. He fanned through my papers quickly, almost as if he were looking for something hidden between the pages. "All right," he said. "Open the back of the truck, please."

"Don't you want to take a look at—"

"Open—the—back," he said again.

"Of course." I cut the engine, got down from the cab and followed him around to the rear, with Todd not far behind me.

I could hear George's tail thumping as we approached. I unlatched the door, and before opening it said, "Just so you know, my dog is back here. He's a big boy and a little cautious around men." He nodded and I pushed the door up.

George sat upright inside his crate. He was looking out at us, his droopy eyes sparkling with excitement and his tail still thumping underneath him. I glanced over at the stern customs officer, to find he had become a different person at the sight of George. His face had softened and he was even smiling.

"Wow, what a beautiful dog! What's his name?"

"George."

"Hello, George," he said, taking a step forward and raising his arm toward the crate before second-guessing himself. "Why is he cautious around men? He doesn't look aggressive."

"No, he's not aggressive, just a bit . . . worried. He was rescued."

"Poor guy. I'm not going to hurt you, buddy," he said as he extended his hand toward George's crate. George cautiously sniffed it. "I love dogs," the officer said.

"So do I," said Todd, with sarcasm that only I understood.

"He sure is beautiful. He seems like a nice dog, and you have your papers for yourself and him. Everything looks good. Have a safe drive."

The whole exchange took all of three minutes. I was surprised.

I climbed back into the driver's seat and the customs officer got

back in his booth. "Here you go," he told me, handing back our passports and my stack of documents and giving us a little wave through.

"Don't you need to stamp all this or something?"

"No, you're fine. You can deal with all that later when you get to California."

I shrugged. "All right then. Thanks." I put the truck into drive and off we went.

"Looks like someone other than you likes the dog," Todd said.

"Maybe *you* should try liking him. You two have a lot in common."

Todd stared at me like I was nuts. "Really. And how's that?"

"You're both very big. You're both very nice to me. And you both make me laugh."

"Hmm, whatever." Todd said, as he gazed out the window.

"I would say you are both *exactly* alike, but George is way smarter."

Todd tried his best not to laugh as we pulled onto the Michigan interstate and headed to California.

THIRTEEN

T he drive continued smoothly the next day—for a while. The scenery was beautiful, Todd and I were carrying on our normal animated conversations and George seemed to be managing well. He was starting to recognize that Todd was a constant part of our pack and was warming up to him on our pit stops. George never met a telephone pole he didn't like and made a big production of marking them at every gas station or roadside rest area we visited.

"That dog pees like a racehorse," Todd said, as George lifted his leg for what seemed an eternity.

"We all have our talents," I said.

Todd looked down at George, "You know, after a few beers or a couple of coffees, I can pee like that, too. Tomorrow morning I'll show you who can pee the longest, George."

George stared up at him and wagged his tail. I rolled my eyes and shook my head, though secretly I was glad they were starting to get along.

In the early evening, somewhere in the expanse of western Iowa, I got a call from my Toronto real estate agent to let me know that the house had sold—Jane's and mine. We got over the asking price. I was

pleased. Todd and I celebrated at an old roadside diner by ordering a couple of pulled-pork sandwiches, which we ate at a rickety picnic table as the sun set over the cornfields, a John Mellencamp song echoing through the open windows of the diner. Here we were, in the heart of America, me with my dog and my best friend. Without asking me, Todd threw George a hunk of meat from his sandwich. I never fed George table scraps, but in this circumstance I made an exception.

"He likes it!" Todd exclaimed. "You know, he is actually a pretty nice dog. I can see why you like him so much. He's good for you."

"You think?" I asked, eyeing George, who was waving his big tail. "Yeah, you're right. He *is* good for me."

"I'm going to miss you, you know. But you deserve to be happy again. California will be good for you . . . and for George," Todd said, and punched me hard on the arm, really hard.

"What the . . . ? That hurt!"

"You're such a tough guy," Todd said. "Come on, George. Let's get a move on." Then he picked up George's leash and walked toward the truck with him as if he were the biggest dog lover in the world.

By the time we packed it in on Wednesday night, just across the Colorado border, George had endured three long driving days. We'd tried to be as mindful as possible—stopping every few hours to walk him, give him more food and water and hugs, play with him a bit and make sure he was comfortable. But we still had a lot of driving left ahead of us.

On the fourth morning—a clear, beautiful day—George's head was dropped forward and he was not making eye contact with me. He enacted a "sitting protest" before finally relenting and jumping into the

travel crate. I was getting better at reading his facial expressions and posture, and for the first time on the trip I got the sense he wasn't happy. George had had enough.

We drove for about ninety minutes and then stopped for a walk. Afterward, as we approached the truck, instead of another sitting protest, George decided to make a break for it and pulled away without warning, yanking the leash out of my hand. Fortunately Todd stopped him and redirected him toward the vehicle, but even with the two of us working in tandem, we couldn't get George to go back in his crate.

"George, sit." Instead he jumped and dodged both Todd and me, moving just out of arm's reach, his tail wagging like this was a really fun game.

"Get that donut he likes!" Todd yelled over at me as George spun around the truck.

"That's not going to work," I said. "He's making a statement. He's trying to say he's had enough of the crate."

"Great. I'm not spending all day playing tag with your dog. What are we going to do?"

It was a good question. I didn't have an answer. George was standing about five feet away from us, eyes wide and alert. He took a few tentative steps forward. Todd whispered, "He's coming toward you." It was like we were trying to trap a bear or some other wild game animal, not a big, galumphing domestic dog.

George got a bit closer and I firmly grabbed his collar. "And that's just about enough, George," I said. He knew the game was over, so this time he engaged in passive resistance, lying down on his back, belly up, becoming a huge, furry dead weight. No matter how I coaxed him or tried to lift him, he remained limp and heavy. Except his tail. He wagged it slowly the whole time, as proof of his sense of humor.

"Now what?" Todd asked.

"I have no idea."

Todd shook his head as he gazed down at the giant sprawled dog, who refused to get up. "I can't believe the crazy crap you get me into."

"Hey, this was your idea," I said. "You wanted to come on this road trip."

Then, together Todd and I lifted the 140 lb. limp, dead weight of George into the cab. "I never knew fur could weigh so much," he said, as we maneuvered George into the crate.

We must have looked ridiculous. George had a little gleam in his eye that told me he thought this was all hilarious, and when we closed the door of the crate, he jumped up, wagging his tail like he hadn't had that much fun in ages.

Todd took the wheel for the next stretch and we didn't say much for the first hour or so. As we started to drive through the Rockies and the road climbed, the sun was beating down on us and the temperature was rising. "We need to pull over," I said.

Todd glanced at me, confused.

"I'm worried about George. It's getting hot outside. I have to make sure he's okay."

"Colin, there's traffic. This isn't the best place to stop, and you know he'll be hard to get back in the truck."

"I know, and that's too bad, but we're stopping anyway," I said.

"All right." Todd pulled the truck over to the shoulder and put on the hazard lights. When I let George out, he was panting and wagging his tail. We gave him a good long drink of water, and when he was done, I broke the news to Todd: "He's not getting back in that crate."

"What are you talking about?"

"I'm not putting him back there again, Todd. I would rather be over-cautious. I don't want him to get too hot."

"So, where exactly is he going then?"

"He's riding up front with us."

Todd stared at me like I was out of my mind. "I am not riding with . . . with that mountain of fur and slobber breathing down my neck from here to California. Nope. No way. Besides, he'll never fit. The jump seat is too small."

"I'll get him to lie on the floor on the passenger side."

"Colin. For real? Can't you see we're not dealing with a tiny frou-frou dog here—he's huge!"

I turned to George, who was lying in the shade of the truck as cars sped loudly by us, only feet away on the interstate.

"I'm not riding with him in my lap," Todd added.

"He needs to stay cool," I said.

George looked as exasperated as we were.

"Fine," Todd said, still angry but relenting. "But I'm driving the rest of the way. You manage the dog."

"All right. Fine," I said. "I'm sorry about this, but there's no other choice."

"Let's just get going."

Todd took his place in the driver's seat, and I closed up the back and led George around to the passenger side. I opened the door and George immediately hopped up, as happy and obliging as could be. He settled right into the front seat.

"No, George," I said. "You're going down here." I patted the floor mat to show him where to lie. He eyed me for a second and then dropped his front paws onto the mat, so that his entire rear end was up high and his giant tail was fanning Todd's face.

"Nice. Very nice," Todd said, as he brought up his arms in defense.

"Okay, so this isn't going to work."

Todd pretend-coughed "Told you so" into his hand. George lifted

his front paws back up onto the passenger seat to regain his regal pose. He tossed Todd a victorious look over his shoulder.

"Wait," I said, leaving the two of them and going around to the rear of the truck.

I fished out a sleeping bag and went back to the cab, climbed in and around George—no easy feat—and set about constructing a makeshift dog bed for George on the tiny, low jump seat.

"What are you doing?" Todd asked, as this time it was my rear end getting far too close to his face.

"Just give me a second."

Todd sighed and leaned into the door. Meanwhile, George showed his gratitude at being up front the best way he knew how: by licking my face and neck while I lowered the jump seat and laid the sleeping bag on top of it. With George's invaluable help I eventually managed to make a serviceable spot. Covered in dog slobber, we set off. As we drove, it became apparent he couldn't really sit on it (because the motion of the truck would throw him off balance), nor could he comfortably lie on it (because it was too small), so he ended up positioning himself in a spread eagle, half on top of me in the passenger seat and half on the jump seat. George was delighted and quite comfortable. Todd was not.

That setup lasted about forty-five minutes. It ended when I finally realized that my cherished friendship with Todd would be over forever if I didn't do something.

"Okay, pull off," I said.

And that's when I came to terms with the last available option. Leaving George in the passenger seat, I took my place on the cramped, hard jump seat, which even though it was much lower than the captain's seats, was easier for me to sit on than it was for George. Sandwiched between my giant dog and my equally giant friend, I looked like a small, helpless child. I felt ridiculous, which wasn't helped

by Todd turning to look down at me every few minutes, grinning and saying things like "How's it going down there?" Meantime, George sat comfortably on the passenger seat. I had cracked the window a bit, and he stuck his head out, face, cheeks and ears blowing in the breeze; he was loving it.

We rode like that all the way down the western slope of the Rockies, through Utah and into Nevada. Todd did all the driving, all the way to California, in that same ridiculous configuration: George and Todd perched high on their thrones, surveying the world beyond the windshield as if they claimed dominion over it—and me with my head just barely visible over the dashboard. I tried to look on the bright side: at least no one in my new neighborhood would see me.

FOURTEEN

The sudden increase in traffic was our warm welcome to Los Angeles, California. I learned quickly that the legendary chaos of L.A. traffic was not exaggerated. We exited the congested freeway and drove toward my new home in Hermosa Beach. As we approached, we could see the palm trees that lined Pier Avenue, and pretty girls floating by on skateboards, while surfers in wet suits made their way to the beach. We must have seemed an odd sight, jammed together in the cab, clunking down the street in our beat-up truck, Todd driving, George with his big head lolling out the window and drool blowing off his tongue—and me in between, barely peering over the dash.

Todd looked over at George. "You're not in Kansas anymore, Toto," he said. George was busy staring at pedestrians who had stopped and were pointing and staring at us. This was a much different neighborhood from the one we'd left in Toronto just a few days before. There were quaint surf shops and restaurants teeming with tanned, happy people. Beyond the street was the beautiful beach, full of surfers and volleyball players and families relaxing and soaking up the sun. The beach looked even nicer than the photos of it I'd seen online. "What

do you think, George?" I asked. He turned to me for a moment, sending a thread of sticky drool onto my shirt. "Thanks, buddy."

We arrived at a complex of town houses where my new apartment was located, just two blocks away from the beach. We parked the truck out front and George pawed at the front seat, eager to get out. "Hold your horses there, big guy," I said, putting him on the leash and guiding him down from his passenger-side throne. He burst forth and promptly peed on the first palm tree he found. Todd and I stretched our legs a bit and then climbed the stairs up to my unit, with George bounding up the stairs behind us.

I opened the front door to a huge loft space. The bedroom was on the second floor, overlooking a living room with soaring twenty-foot ceilings. A double set of French doors led to a small balcony. "Wow, this is pretty nice," Todd said as we walked out and took in the courtyard below, with a swimming pool surrounded by palm trees.

"What do you think, George?" I asked. He was wagging his tail and eyeing the pool as though he wanted to jump right in.

Todd decided to start unloading the truck while I took George for a walk in his new neighborhood. "I need to stretch his legs," I said. "We'll be back shortly."

"No problem. Do what you gotta do."

George bounced up and down with excitement when I clipped on his leash and told him we were going for a walk. We headed down to the street and had only gone about fifteen feet, when the ocean breeze hit us. I closed my eyes and took a deep breath. No matter where I am on earth or what ocean I'm beside, that smell does the same thing to me: it takes me back to my grandfather's cottage as a kid. I looked down at George, who was standing stock-still beside me. His head pointed skyward and his big nose was twitching, breathing the fresh ocean air.

"Come on, George. Let's go see the beach."

As we walked a block down the hill, the big Pacific Ocean waves came into view. Sunbathers, surfers and lifeguard stands dotted the beach. We crossed Hermosa Avenue onto the paved path known as the Strand. I loved the Strand right away. It felt like a Beach Boys song coming to life. As far as the eye could see, animated people, most wearing surf shorts, bathing suits or lululemon gear, walked, ran, skateboarded or cycled. "See all the people, George?" I said, but when I faced him, George was oblivious. The only thing he was looking at was the water, which was only sixty yards of pure white sand away.

"All right. Let's go check it out, big guy."

In a split second an incredible transformation took place. Here was a dog, a Landseer Newfoundland—for generations bred to be the most powerful, web-footed, fearless, water-savvy dog on earth—seeing and smelling the ocean for the very first time. As he gazed at the water, his genetic hardwiring, unspoken and instinctive, reached George's brain. So what did he do?

He bolted.

He pulled the leash out of my hand and left me standing on the Strand, helplessly watching. He ran faster than I have ever seen any dog run. He ran past the sunbathing teenagers. He ran past college students playing beach volleyball. He ran past little kids with plastic buckets and shovels building sand castles. He ran with the singular purpose of making it to the water.

"George!" I called, but I knew it was pointless. My one hope was that when he got to the shoreline and saw up close the huge waves with their walls of water crashing toward him, he would get scared and stop. After all, he'd never seen an ocean. I walked at a leisurely pace to catch up to him. Before I was even close, he reached the shore . . . and kept going, throwing himself headlong into the oncoming surf.

"Oh no," I muttered. Then I yelled, "George!" He ignored me completely, catapulting himself through the surf and swimming out to sea, his attention fixed on something far out in the water. I shielded my eyes against the sun and spotted a handful of surfers past the break. They were about thirty-five yards from shore, lying on their boards and waiting for the next set of big waves to roll in. George was beelining for the closest one.

"No, George! Stop! Come back!" He had swum out about fifteen yards or so, but he was still in the wash that rushes to shore after a wave breaks. He hadn't yet been hit by the full force of a big wave. The next thing I saw was a large wave curl and break in front of him, kicking up a solid four-foot wall of white water. Surely when that wall of water hit him he would go under and get rolled, and that would be enough to send him swimming back to shore.

But that's not what happened. When the white water surged and hit him, sure enough he completely disappeared underneath the froth. I felt a jolt of panic and picked up my pace. By the time I reached the water's edge, his head had popped back up. He didn't look at all panicked. He refocused on the surfers beyond the break and kept swimming out to them with determination. "George! This way!" I cried, waving my arms and beckoning him back to shore. He looked like a tugboat churning through rough water. By this point he had cleared the white water and was out deeper, where another big, rolling wave was about to break on him. I felt fear in the pit of my stomach. Even if I dived in and swam my hardest, there was no way I'd make it to him in time.

I looked out beyond George's bobbing head, where the surfers were now taking notice of the massive dog swimming toward them. A few had lifted themselves onto their boards to get a better view. "It's a dog, a biggie!" Now they were all up on their boards,

pointing and laughing and directing all attention to George. "What's he doing?" one of them shouted. Another one said, "He's coming this way!"

The wave rolled in. George paddled up its face—all seven feet of it—somehow keeping his head high above the surface. He hung on the crest for a brief, majestic moment before the wave rolled over him, pushing him down, and submerging him. This was it: George was in trouble. He had been hit by a huge wave and he was going to drown before my very eyes. And there was nothing I could do to stop it.

A few seconds later, to my great relief, his head popped to the surface as though it was a cork. He was okay! In fact, he appeared even more intent on swimming farther out instead of heading to shore. His paws cycled rapidly, and his instinct carried him out over the next crest, right to the group of surfers. By this point they'd all given up on catching a wave themselves and were focused solely on George. George zeroed in on the nearest one—a blond, lanky boy on an orange-and-white surfboard. George swam in a direct line to him. When it became clear which surfer he was headed for, the target started yelling at me, "Du-u-de! Get your dog!"

How in the world was I going to do that? I didn't have time to think. Instead I took off my T-shirt, fished my wallet out of my shorts and piled both, along with George's leash, on top of my flip-flops in the sand. I ran into the water and waded out, shouting George's name, hoping he would hear me and turn around. After a few more seconds George made it to the board, which the blond surfer was lying on like a seal, belly down. George grabbed the surfer's arm in his mouth. "Hey!" the kid yelled. "Let go!" At first I thought George might be biting him. But the next thing I saw was that George had changed directions, and as he began pulling the

kid on the board toward shore, the kid started laughing and pushing George away. The big Newf was not easily deterred, and his head kept popping back up to the surface, no matter how many times the kid pushed him away.

I called for George again—to no avail. Then I dived under a big wave and emerged safely on the other side, much closer to him now. At this point George had stopped trying to drag the surfer to shore and instead had thrown his front paws on the surfer's board and was trying to climb on. "Du-u-de!" the surfer said to George. "Get your own board!" All the other surfers were howling with laughter, but the loudest laugh of all came from the kid being attacked by the great white-and-black fur shark beside him. "Your dog's a board hog!" the kid yelled my way. He gave George yet another push back into the water. "He's killing my joy here, du-u-de!"

"Sorry, I'm getting him!" I shouted as I swam. Finally George had heard me and he turned toward my voice. Abandoning the surfers, he started swimming straight for me, his eyes wide with excitement.

"Good boy, George. Come this way!"

Over the years I have watched a few dogs swim at the beach or in lakes, chasing balls and sticks, but this was unlike anything I'd ever seen. Even at a distance I could tell that George didn't swim using the standard "doggie paddle." Instead he thrust one paw at a time out in front of him and then pulled it to the side of his body and down, catapulting himself forward in powerful bursts. It was similar to a breast stroke used by competitive swimmers. He kept his head up high in the water and moved toward me with the steady determination of a rescue boat.

California waves are long and smooth, not like the shorter, sporadic Atlantic-coast waves I'd grown up with. "George, watch out!"

I yelled, as a new, big, Pacific wave approached him. He was right in the trough now and luckily had good timing, as it swelled and carried him along. He actually bodysurfed for a few yards before he slipped behind the crest and the wave broke in front of him. He swam through the white water, his ears up and his eyes wide, and the next thing I knew he was right beside me.

"George!" I said, breathless. "What are you doing?" This close I could see what I'd failed to see earlier: there was no panic in his eyes, and George was having the time of his life. He took my arm in his mouth, the same thing he'd tried to do with the surfer. He wasn't holding hard enough to break the skin—it was more a steady grip than a bite—but his teeth held firm. I let him lead me a ways to shore, but when the water was back down to my mid thigh and his paws hit the bottom, he wouldn't stop pulling. And now he was pulling with enough force that it started to hurt. "George, no!" I said, trying to push him away. He didn't listen.

When we finally made it to shore, he let go of me, shook off a geyser of spray and then stood looking at me, wagging his tail furiously. As I bent over to catch my breath, he licked my face as hard as he could. He was obviously proud of pulling me out of the water. I held his collar with my good arm—the one not covered in pink teeth marks—and led him over to where I'd piled my things. He didn't walk over—he pranced, lifting his front paws high the way show horses do. He was as happy and excited and alive as I'd ever seen him. I let myself fall onto the sand, still holding tight to his collar.

"That was crazy! You had me worried. I didn't know you could swim like that." He unleashed a flurry of kisses on my head.

"George," I said. "You're supposed to come when I call. And you can't grab people on surfboards." I was both concerned and upset that he had run away from me like that, but at the same time, I'd just

witnessed this dog's first-ever swim, and clearly he'd just discovered the thing he'd been born and bred to do. It was amazing.

George was prancing again, alternating between his two front paws in what can only be described as a dance of joy. My reprimand was falling on deaf, wet ears.

I got him back on the leash and kept him close as I slipped my shirt over my head. A woman walking briskly toward us called out, "Excuse me! You! Excuse me!"

She was in her late thirties, wearing giant black sunglasses and a thin purple wrap over her bathing suit. "You're not supposed to have dogs on the beach!" she said, raising her voice.

On Nova Scotia beaches dogs could come and go as they pleased. "I'm sorry—I had no idea," I said.

"Your dog is dangerous. I saw him biting you!" She looked at George, who now sat obediently by my side and had lowered his head and turned the other way when he heard her raised voice. She gestured to a post on which a massive sign outlined the bylaw banning dogs from the beach and warning of a fine. Only then did I notice these signs were posted on every fourth or fifth pole all the way down the beach.

"Look, I'm sorry," I said. "He wasn't biting me. He's a water-rescue dog, and he was just trying to rescue the surfers . . . We're not from here. I didn't see the sign. I'm sorry."

"You missed that?" she said, pointing at the sign right beside us.

"I guess so, yeah."

"What if that thing had latched on to—"

I interrupted her before she could finish. "Sorry. Really. You've made your point. We're leaving now." I picked up my flip-flops and wallet and dragged a very reluctant George away from the water.

As we were going, the surfers called out, "See ya later, George!"

We walked back to the apartment, both of us dripping wet and covered in sand. Todd was waiting by the truck as we approached.

"What the hell happened to you two?" he asked.

"Don't ask. It's a long story."

FIFTEEN

Todd had to be back home for a work commitment, so the next day George and I drove him to the airport in the moving truck for his flight to Toronto.

"That was a hell of a road trip," Todd said as we stepped out of the truck onto the curb of Terminal 2 at LAX. I had George's leash in my hand. Todd looked down at George and reached out to rub his head. "I never thought I would say this, but you're a good boy, George. You watch out for my friend, okay?"

"I will," I said.

"Not you. I was talking to George."

George leaned into Todd's hand and wagged his tail. Todd then turned to me and gave me a big hug, and amid the smell of jet fuel and the roar of airplanes landing and taking off, he said, "You're a great friend. I love you, man. I'm going to miss you." Then he slapped me on the back a couple of times, picked up his bag and walked into the terminal.

I didn't know what to say. Guys don't say things like that to each other. I've never said anything like that to any of my friends, but after nearly twenty-five years of friendship, shared dreams and a few

failures, Todd felt compelled to utter what I couldn't. It was so good to hear his words.

After he entered the terminal, I bent down to hug George and felt a few tears running down my face. I knew I would miss my friend very much. George licked my cheek and I nuzzled his shoulder. A few seconds later I felt a tap on my back and pivoted to find one of L.A.'s finest peering down at me.

"Sir, get the truck and dog out of the way—you're blocking traffic."

"Oh. Sorry. Sure."

George and I hopped into the truck and took off. The drive back to Hermosa Beach was difficult and I found myself wiping more tears off my face. I felt lost, both literally and figuratively. George sat in the passenger seat, and instead of looking out the window the way he usually did, he spent most of his time staring at me. I didn't know where I was or where I was supposed to be going. I didn't know where the grocery stores were—or even what they were called—and I didn't have a single friend in the city who could show me around.

"It's just you and me," I said to George once we got home. I unpacked a few boxes and halfheartedly tried to settle in. George seemed perfectly content with things and sprawled comfortably on the floor, but I felt strange being in this new apartment and not in my normal house. This didn't really change much in the weeks and months that followed. In fact, it only got worse.

I had a wonderful new job, which I loved. Every morning before work I visited the beach, basked in the sunshine and watched pretty girls. I knew I should have been overjoyed at the direction my life had taken. Instead I struggled with the feeling that I didn't "belong." I was emotionally disconnected and I felt homesick, even though I no longer had a home to be sick for. When friends and family called to ask how

I was doing, I said, "I'm great!" How could I complain when I lived in
a paradise mere blocks away from the beach? But the truth was, with-
out knowing it I was slipping into a depression.

George, on the other hand, was taking all the change in stride.
Big dogs aren't common in Los Angeles (Newfoundlands, even less
so) and the attention he got any time we left the house was astound-
ing. In the land of "Hollywood purse dogs" like Chihuahuas and
teacup poodles, big, black-and-white George stood out from the pack.
It was next to impossible to walk even a few blocks without being
stopped and George being fussed over. Almost everybody noticed
him—middle-aged couples, retirees, rock stars and celebrities, young
beach volleyball players, surfers, skateboarders and groups of Asian
tourists. From as far as half a block away I'd hear "Oh my god! He's
beautiful!" and "What kind of dog is he?" I was having the same
"basic facts" conversation—"He's a Newfoundland. His name's
George. He's a rescue. He's friendly"—twenty or more times a day.

George began to lose his introversion, even around men. It was
as though he suddenly picked up on how special he was and started to
gain self-confidence. He developed new tricks and go-to moves I'd
never seen before. If folks hugged him, he licked their faces. And when
they loved it, the next person who hugged him would get licked twice
as hard. People took photos and George would patiently pose, his head
held high for the camera.

I also saw that he was a magnet for women. The rumors and
legends of beautiful California girls are all true, and many of these
women, often in tiny bikinis, would approach us, or rather George.
"Can we pet your dog? He is so big and fluffy! Can we hug him?"

I would stammer, "Sure. I'm sure he'd love that," and then stand
there and watch my dog receive the kind of attention most red-blooded
guys only dream of. I wasn't jealous, but it was a bit weird.

One time, as he was being patted and admired by a group of attractive, bikini-clad women, he flipped on his back and let them rub his belly. The ladies let out a collective "Aw-w-w-w-w" and got down on their knees to scratch and tickle him, while George closed his eyes and blissfully stretched out to his full length—about six-and-a-half feet— on the sidewalk. Flipping onto his back soon became one of his favorite moves, and people loved it. Some days he spent more time lying on his back than walking.

What set George apart from other dogs, though, was the special interest he was now taking in children or anyone he perceived as weak or vulnerable. Parents would approach and ask, "Can my kids pet him?"

"Of course," I'd say. "He's very friendly." Kids' faces were at George's eye level, and he loved that. He would gently look children in the eye before offering up a slobbering, affectionate kiss on the cheek.

"Mom, he's a teddy bear!" I'd hear as kids squealed in surprise. And when parents would inevitably have to draw their kids away before they wanted to leave, I'd hear "Bye, George!" and "You're the best dog ever, George!" or even "George, I love you!" Sometimes it was the adults making the comments, not just the children. George heard these things, too, and it was obvious the gentle giant was thriving on all the attention. Something in him was healing. He was becoming a happy new dog. He was becoming George.

As George was coming into himself, I continued to feel less and less like myself. Despite feeling disconnected, I made a conscious effort to get out on the weekends and explore. Of course George helped motivate me—he approached every day as a new adventure. He suddenly wanted to do things with me, go out and live life, and he forced me to

come along for the ride. When he jumped up on the bed Saturday mornings, wagging his tail and looking at me like "Let's go! Let's go for a walk! Let's go for a drive! Let's go down to the beach! Come on!" he was impossible to resist. He was always excited to head out into the world. It was always nice outside, so I had no excuse. He made it easier for me to click into that same headspace.

Someone at the office had told me about a place the locals called Dog Beach. It was a two-mile stretch of Huntington Beach in Orange County, just north of the famous pier. Dogs were not only permitted, they were allowed to roam leash free. I threw some towels, water bottles and an umbrella beside George in the back of our new SUV, and we drove down to check the beach out.

I hoped George would get a chance to swim and enjoy the water without worrying about rules or disrupting surfers and families the way he had that first day in Hermosa Beach. We arrived to find the beach populated with a ton of dogs of every breed and size, and the same could have been said for their owners. When George caught sight of the beach, his tail beat against the seat of the SUV like he was banging on a big bass drum. I parked, opened the back, and George leaped out, ready to go. "George," I said. "I need you to be on your best behavior, okay?"

As we approached the beach, George pulled on the leash excitedly. Once we were at the beach I said, "Sit," and after some protest and straining, he eventually gave me his attention and plopped his rear end on the sand. "Good boy!"

We took a moment to survey the scene—two miles of beautiful white sand with big Pacific Ocean waves rolling in. Everywhere around us dogs chased balls and sticks into the surf, lounged with their owners under giant umbrellas, ran around in yipping packs, dug at the sand, herded each other, swam and sniffed butt. George and I both loved the chaos right away.

"This looks great, George!" I said, as his tail swished a sand angel behind him.

Making sure there were no surfers or swimmers in the water in front of us he might try to "rescue," I unclipped his leash and drew in a deep breath. "Okay, go play!" I said, hoping he wouldn't cause disaster and destruction as he took off like a rocket across the beach and into the ocean.

As it turned out, he loved playing with the other wet, sloppy beach dogs—running, wrestling, swimming and chasing seagulls. In Toronto he hadn't quite known how to play with other dogs and would only watch the social sequences from afar. At Dog Beach that started to change. George clumsily reciprocated the playful advances of other dogs. Even though he was by far the largest on the beach, George was gentle and submissive with big and small dogs alike.

The surfers down the beach weren't too fazed when George swam out to say hi. "What's his name?" one kid waiting for a wave called out to me. I told him, and he patted George's big, wet head as George circled his board.

It got to the point where the local surfers all knew George and would greet him when we arrived. "Hey, George! Surf's up!" I'd hear, and George would gallop into the water and eagerly swim out to greet them. Often I'd join George in the water, and that's how we learned to swim together. George and I liked to swim in the flatter water away from the shore, out beyond the constant break of the surf and churning white water.

It was on one of these swims, late on a warm, windless, sunny Saturday, with George right beside me that I looked down and saw a large, black torpedo shape streak underneath us. "What the . . . ?" I said, startled. I glanced over at George, who was placidly swimming along and hadn't seen a thing. I scanned the water and spotted a

telltale triangular dorsal fin break the surface just ahead. A big knot instantly formed in the pit of my stomach—the object was a shark.

I turned to George. "George! Come!" He must have sensed my urgency, because he picked up speed and swam right over to my side. Just then another dorsal fin broke the surface, but this time a loud exhale of mist and air accompanied it. "George. It's a dolphin!" I said with a huge sense of relief and excitement. George's wet ears perked right up, and as we looked all around us, dorsal fins surfaced from all directions and loud exhales sounded. An entire pod of curious Pacific bottlenose dolphins encircled us.

George was equally curious and delighted, and swam toward each one as it broke the surface. At one point several of the larger dolphins slowed and lifted their heads out of the water to get a clearer view of the big, hairy dog fearlessly churning toward them. George called out with one of his rare, deep barks, and this brought them even closer—so close I thought George would be nose to nose with them at any moment. It was incredible and I was smiling so much that swimming seemed effortless.

The dozen or so dolphins cavorted around George and me for two or three minutes before they continued on their path northward along the beach. George tried to follow them, and for a moment I was struck by the image of the sleek water creatures, with their smooth, slippery, gray skin, and their odd adopted land sibling weighed down by a thick, furry black-and-white coat.

Eventually George did a U-turn in the water and paddled back my way, with an expression on his face that can only be described as wonder. I expect my face looked about the same.

When we got back to the shore, George shook himself off and then stared out to sea where the dolphins had swum away. His eyes were wide and he pranced in the sand, his front paws sending up spray in his wake.

"You made some new friends, George. Maybe they'll be back next week." George wagged his tail and we made our way up the beach to the SUV.

As we got settled in the vehicle, the sun and sand still on us, it occurred to me that we'd had a near-perfect day, maybe even a "free day." I looked back through the rearview mirror at George. His happy face and serene eyes said it all. He was content. Yet, while this pleased me and I could recognize it logically, I couldn't feel happy or content myself. I had all the reasons in the world to, but somehow I still felt emotionally disconnected. Only one question remained: why?

In the inexplicable fog I was in, I started to pay careful attention to George and his blooming confidence. Maybe if I watched him, I would learn something about how to be happy. Maybe if I acted like George did, I could feel good, too. It was worth a try.

Over the next few weeks I observed George. I studied how he treated everyone he met. Whether he was being patted by someone wealthy who'd just stepped out of a Bentley or by a down-and-out street person, he was the same: he was just George.

"You can't buy friends," my grandfather always used to say. Like George, he was great with people and everyone loved him. When I was a kid and feeling unhappy about things at home, he would put his arm around me and talk in a soft voice. "It's the simple things in life that matter most, like watching big clouds floating in the blue sky, like the smell of fresh-cut hay or the sound of waves against the shore." His encouragement still echoed in my adult head: "Don't worry about things being perfect. Be happy with doing your best, and the rest will come." As I watched George behaving first like a normal dog and later

as a beacon of light to everyone and everything around him, I couldn't help but wonder, Why don't I feel normal? Is there a way to be more like George?

Then one day George and I were on our usual walk in our neighborhood, when we came upon an old man sitting on the sidewalk. He was in pretty rough shape, his face weather-beaten and drawn. There aren't a lot of homeless people on the streets of Hermosa Beach, so this guy stood out. He had a couple of garbage bags and a beat-up hat beside him, filled with small change. The sign by his hat read "Vietnam veteran. Homeless. Please help."

George was out in front of me as we came upon him. "George, walk with me," I quietly said so he would not disturb the man sitting there. George had other ideas and he pulled forward on the leash right up to the homeless man and gave him a lick on his face.

"Sorry," I said, as I tried to tug George back.

The man took some distance from George for a second to get a better look at him. He smiled and said, "That's okay." To George he added, "You're a big dog, aren't you?"

George's tail swished behind him and he leaned into the man, something he only did when he was really comfortable with someone. In response the man chuckled and threw an arm around him, pulling him into a side hug as if George were one of his old buddies.

"You sure are beautiful, aren't you?" After a while the man looked up at me. "What kind of dog is he?"

I told him.

"Not many people are friendly to me. But you're real friendly," he said. George started licking the man's face again.

"Sorry," I said. "He can be a little too friendly sometimes."

"No, no." The man hugged George. "It's okay. I like it." He scratched George behind the ears and George's leg started thumping.

George proffered another lick on the cheek, and then he looked up at me as if to say, "I made another friend. Isn't he great?"

George could have sat with that homeless guy all day. In fact, I'm sure he would have, but it was me who wanted to move along. I felt a bit guilty and awkward, so I fished some money out of my pocket.

"Here you go," I said, reaching down to pass the man a couple of dollar bills.

"What?" He grabbed my hand and closed my fingers around the bills. "No, man. I don't want your money."

"Please, it's okay."

He ignored me and smiled at George, addressing him, not me. "You just gave me something so special," he said. "Do you know that no one's kissed me in years? Most people don't even want to come anywhere near me." He patted George's head, and on cue George licked his face yet again.

"You see?" the man said, his eyes welling with tears. "This is way better than money, man. You keep those bills. You buy him a treat." He gave George one last squeeze and then said, "I think your owner wants to go, buddy, so you better be off."

I gave a light tug on the leash and George stood up.

"You take care of him." It took me a while to realize he'd directed those last words at George, not at me.

PART FOUR

Surfing with George

SIXTEEN

I was seventeen years old, and when I wasn't spending time with my grandfather at his cottage, I was lifeguarding at Rissers Beach in Nova Scotia. Rissers Beach is not exactly a surfer's paradise. In fact, back then no one surfed in Nova Scotia. There were no surfboards for sale locally and no internet to order one online.

The waves at Rissers Beach aren't the long, smooth-faced, rolling works of art like the waves in California. Quite the opposite. At Rissers Beach big, rideable waves are more abrupt and random, and the water from the North Atlantic is much colder than the Pacific Ocean water off Southern California.

That summer, the Parks service sent all us lifeguards on a special surf-rescue course where they introduced a surfboard to be used as a life-saving tool at the beach. Imported from Australia, it was a clunky thing, about eleven feet long and wide enough to allow you to haul another person onto it during an emergency. As professionally-trained lifeguards, we took our role seriously. We needed to be fully prepared, so every day we practiced rescuing each other from the cold Atlantic Ocean, paddling out to "save" a panicked or unconscious "victim," hauling the person onto the long board and then navigating back to shore through the pounding surf.

But one stormy day, with big waves and no patrons on the beach, I decided I would give the board a try, not as a rescue tool but as a surfboard. I grabbed the giant board and off I went.

I needed a few tries to get the hang of it, but once I figured out the timing and managed to stand up, the ride was great. I caught a wave about forty yards from shore, surged along its face until it broke and then let the white water carry me back to shore. The whole ride couldn't have lasted more than ten seconds, but it was magic. I was hooked on surfing! I spent my next three summers at Rissers Beach with my fellow lifeguard and friend, Mike, paddling out whenever the swells and a lack of swimmers allowed it. Unfortunately, after university when I moved away to Toronto, I had to abandon the sport. My relocation to Los Angeles decades later, however, presented a great opportunity to pick surfing up again, especially once George found his groove at Dog Beach. He didn't need as much supervision anymore. He no longer insisted on "rescuing" every person and animal near or in the water, and he learned to socialize with other dogs as they played in the waves. Now that I could let him swim and roam freely, it occurred to me: I could get a surfboard.

I often visited Bruce Jones's Surf Shop about five miles up the Pacific Coast Highway from Huntington Beach in Sunset Beach. Bruce was a surf legend who'd been shaping boards since the 1960s, and every time George and I drove home from Dog Beach, we stopped at Bruce's to rinse the sand off George with the shop's hose. We met all the surfers who congregated at the shop at the end of the day, and not surprisingly, all of them, including Bruce, loved George. This side stop became part of our weekend routine.

When I finally rented a board from Bruce, I settled on a big cruiser like the one I'd used at Rissers Beach. It was about eleven feet long. It was not particularly maneuverable and wouldn't have been

good in very big waves, but it was stable and buoyant—a nice board for easing back into the sport.

"George, you don't need me to babysit you anymore," I said when we arrived at Dog Beach at ten one weekend morning. "You stay on the beach and play. I'm going surfing."

The beach was relatively empty that day. There was a light wind and by California standards the waves were small and a bit mushy. It was a perfect day for trying to get my sea legs back. Only a few surfers were already in the water, waiting for the next set of waves to roll in.

I put up our usual umbrella home base and then let George off his leash. "Go have fun, big guy!" I said, though I really didn't need to. George was off in a flash, and was soon cavorting in the waves and meeting every dog and human being in sight. He made friends with a young lab pup and didn't seem to be causing anyone grief, so I figured it was as good a time as any for me to go try surfing again. I settled the board under my arm, carried it to the edge of the sand and launched it into the water. When the water reached my waist, I hopped on and began to paddle out.

I was so fixated on the board and the waves that I didn't notice the exact moment George spotted me in the water. When he did, though, he abandoned the lab pup and swam for me like his life depended on it. Before I knew it, he was chugging alongside me. "Hey, George," I said. "I'm fine. Go back to the beach and have fun." But he was having none of it. As we approached the end of the white water, he was still right beside me. "Come on, George. Go back," I said. "Turn around." Not a chance. He continued swimming with great determination parallel to my board.

The break at Huntington was farther out than at Hermosa, so we were about fifty yards from shore when the first clean waves hit us. You can't duck-dive under waves on a long board because the board is too

big and too buoyant, so when the first wave hit us, I bounced up and over the top of it with George paddling furiously beside me. I knew enough by then not to doubt his swimming abilities, but still, I was concerned about him in the waves.

We blasted up and over, rushing down the opposite side. When we were in the trough with the next wave a couple dozen feet away, I looked at George. "You okay?" I asked. His head was high and he was swimming confidently through the surf. In fact, he looked less tired than I was. He gazed straight ahead, focused on the next wave, but when he noticed me watching him, he adjusted course slightly, bumping his shoulder into the board and rising up out of the water to lick my face. I laughed as he planted kisses on my cheek. I was still laughing and he was still trying to lick me when the next wave hit us.

Distracted by George's show of affection, I had let the board drift, so that instead of being aimed directly up the face of the wave, it was pointed at an angle. When the rush of water lifted us again, the board tilted and I started to slide off its side, which flipped the board skyward and on top of me. I went under and George, also caught off guard, went under with me. I kicked back to the surface, and when I emerged, George was already back up and scanning the water. He spotted me and swam over. He instinctively tried to grab my arm and pull me back to shore the second he was close enough. "I guess you're okay," I said, as I pulled my arm away from him and hoisted myself back on the surfboard. "You're a crazy dog," I added. Before I could paddle out to the lineup, and just as he had with the surfer at Hermosa Beach, George threw his front paws on my board, trying to pull himself onto it.

"Seriously, George?"

He slipped his paws off the right side of the board, briefly went under and then swam around the nose to climb up on my left. He got his head, chest and front paws on the board. Watching him kick at the water

and scramble for grip, I couldn't take it anymore. I grabbed his rear end and helped him onto the board. So there we were: me on the back and George, thrilled to be on the board, wagging his wet tail on the front. I couldn't surf with him on, but I could paddle him back to shore.

"Okay, George. I'll give you a ride back in," I said. "But I'm leaving you there so I can come back out and surf. By myself. Got it?" George wagged his tail in response.

I lay back down on my belly and started stroking through the water with my arms. I thought there was a chance George would jump off when the board began moving, but instead he plopped his rear end down and got comfortable, the water from his wet fur blowing into my face.

"Sit tight, buddy," I said. Even with the two of us on it, the big, floaty board cut through the water efficiently. It wasn't surfing, but I had to admit that paddling George into shore was pretty fun.

A few seconds later I felt a change in the water as it started to draw back toward the open ocean. A wave was closing in at our backs. I thought about shimmying my legs off the back of the board and dragging them behind us as the wave passed but changed my mind when I glanced over my shoulder and saw we were in a perfect position to ride a small, but decently shaped wave. "George!" I said. "Hang on!"

I paddled frantically to match the speed of the wave, and just like that, we were picked up by it. I pulled my arms in, shifting my weight to steer us, and sidled up the back of the board behind George. Even as we gained speed, George didn't move at all. He just sat still, with his chest puffed out and his floppy ears dancing in the wind. And that was it: we were surfing. Sort of. The two of us were moving forward from the energy of the wave!

I started to laugh. "That-a-boy, George!"

I leaned right and we cut back into the wave, parallel to its line, before the wave broke beneath us. We slowed but didn't stop, the white

water swirling in all directions. I dipped my arms in the final fifteen feet and paddled to give us one last surge. The nose of the board caught some backwash, causing George to jolt forward. He turned to glance over his shoulder at me as if to say, "Easy, dude." It looked very much like he was grinning.

We arrived in the shallow water. "This is where you get off, buddy," I said, slipping from the board and a bit out of breath. George eyed me curiously and then hopped into the water as though what we'd just done was no different from climbing a set of stairs. He then waded to shore. When he reached dry sand, he pivoted to me as I dragged the big board up to the beach to meet him. He was wagging his tail so hard his whole back end swung left and right along with it.

"Was that fun?" I asked, as I put the surfboard down.

His wagging massive tail, his panting and his hopping on his two front legs, was as clear an answer as any. He threw his head back and let out a big, deep "Woof."

When I picked up the board and flipped it around so that it pointed back out at the ocean, George ran around me in a circle. And when I walked out and set it down in the water, he immediately jumped back on the front.

Obviously I would not be surfing alone. "All right, George, let's try that again." He thumped his tail.

We went out a second time. George swam beside me until we cleared the break, and then I swung the board around and helped him up, and the two of us caught another wave together and rode it all the way back to shore. Then he hopped off and bounced excitedly up and down, wagging his tail anew, eager to go out again. I, on the other hand, was tired. The two of us were heavy, and paddling with George on board was hard work.

After a short rest we took a third trip out. I noticed some of the local surfers were now watching our runs.

"Dude, your dog is rad!" I heard someone say, and "Man, nice surf buddy you got there!"

Just before noon, when George and I were both tired, we spent some time under the umbrella. One of the surfers approached.

"How'd you train your dog to do that?" he asked.

"I didn't," I told him. "He just jumped on by himself. Today was his first time."

"Whoa! That's so cool! You should put him in the contest."

I looked at him quizzically.

"You don't know about the contest?"

"We just moved here a while back."

"They hold a dog-surfing contest here at the end of September."

"A what?"

"A surfing competition for dogs," he said. "They get a bunch of people out and there are prizes and stuff, and they raise all this money for shelters—like, for rescue dogs."

"He was a rescue," I said, nodding at George. The surfer lit up.

"Me and some buds came last year and had a blast. I mean, mostly it's just funny, but your dog—he's got mad skills. You guys could actually win."

"That sounds kind of crazy, but I'll keep it in mind," I said. "Thanks."

"Seriously. I hope you put him in the contest. It would be awesome."

He waved goodbye and went back to where his friends were waiting for him on the sand. I turned to George. "Hear that, George? He thinks you could win a surfing contest."

George was lying on the blanket under our umbrella. He was covered in sand and soaking wet. His response: snores.

SEVENTEEN

Over the next few months I rented boards from Bruce Jones's almost every weekend. Each time I thought, This is great! I'm going to go surfing on my own today! And each time I found myself out in the water on my board, lying flat on my belly with a giant, wet dog riding high in front of me, looking very much like the figurehead on an ancient tall ship (but with a lot more fur).

I can't say that I wasn't happy with this turn of events, because I was. George and I had found an activity we could do together, one that was "ours" and set us apart from the rest of the world. And that in itself felt great. Plus George got me out of the house, and for the duration that we were in the water, I didn't think about anything at all except the joy of surfing with George. At a time when happiness for me was hard to come by, our weekend excursions were a much-needed source of energy and light.

I'd work all week and be focused and fine at the office, but something in me still felt not quite right. It was like I was going through the motions of life but not really living it. And I was still finding it difficult to establish a social life in L.A. Not that there weren't opportunities; I just didn't know how to manage them. The hurt of my past

still lingered, and I found myself making mistakes when trying to connect with new people. It was a struggle that I kept secret.

My real solace came on weekends when George and I would head to the beach in the morning. "Ready to go?" I'd ask as I took the board down from the SUV.

Wag, wag, wag.

George followed right by my side as we made our way to the shoreline, which was full of dogs and their owners playing in the sand and surf. Instead of joining their antics the way he had before we'd discovered our sport, George focused on me and our banged-up rental surfboard. He'd look me in the eye as if to say, "Time to do our thing."

Out we'd go through the white water, navigating the difficult break and finally reaching the right spot to pick up the waves. We both fell off the board a lot, but even that was fun. We kept to smaller waves at first and eventually, with practice, we began to get better at riding. George started to figure out when to swim close, when to hop on the board, how to balance his weight and leave me room enough to steer us back to shore.

No matter how many times we went out, the excitement of the ride never wore off. Seeing all 140 pounds of Newf sitting regally in front of me, as we glided across the surface of the water, never failed to make me smile. Occasionally George would turn his head, trying to look back at me. I'd catch his face in profile, and he had that expression of serenity you see when a dog hangs its head out a car window. I had to laugh.

At the shore after every single wave, he would find me and lick my face. Every—single—time. Surfing wasn't some novelty act for George. He got on the board because he loved it. He was truly having the time of his life.

Most afternoons after we'd been out for a while, George would nap under the umbrella to escape the worst of the sun. When he did,

I'd creep off as quietly as I could to surf on my own. All dogs pick up on cues—some subtle, some surfboard sized—George appeared to have a tracking device on me. Before I'd made it ten feet into the water, he'd be awake and bounding to the shoreline, right there beside me. Never once did I manage to get a ride in on my own. But the truth is that I didn't really care. I loved to surf with George.

One day, determined to surf by myself, I left him at home when I went to the beach. I rented a smaller board and had an amazing time catching waves, but the whole time I felt guilty. I kept replaying the sad look on his face as he stood by the door when I left my house. It actually seemed wrong that he wasn't with me. This was the first and only time I left him behind.

Over those months at the beach people regularly approached us after we'd been out in the waves. "You guys are amazing!" they'd say. "I've never seen a dog who loves to surf the way yours does. How did you train him?"

"I didn't," I'd respond with a shrug. "He just knows how to do it."

Occasionally I would hear about that dog-surfing competition at Huntington and what a great fund-raiser the event was for shelter dogs.

"Will we see you and George there this year?"

"I'm not sure."

The more I heard about the event, the more unsure I became— big crowds, lots of attention, TV cameras and everyone watching as dogs and their owners took to surfboards to compete against each other. Outside of work events, I wasn't comfortable in crowds and I wasn't sure I wanted to subject George to a competition where there'd be pressure to win. Over the years I'd been ultra-competitive at hockey. I wanted to win every time I stepped on the ice. I didn't feel that way about surfing, which I considered a spiritual or lifestyle activity rather than a competitive sport. I especially didn't feel competitive with

George; I just liked doing things with him quietly and alone. It's how we connected.

Also, after almost three months of living in California I'd finally figured out how to get around, but I still hadn't shaken the core feeling of insecurity. I carried it around with me everywhere. I could focus on new things and new people at work; however, on the weekends I really valued quiet time by myself and with George. A dog-surfing contest certainly didn't qualify as quiet time, and though this didn't quite surface as a conscious thought, it made me uneasy.

But then I was online one day, and I came across a link from the American Society for the Prevention of Cruelty to Animals. I read about the prevalence of "high kill" shelters throughout L.A. and Orange Counties. Hundreds of dogs were being put to death each week simply because the shelters had no room for them or no funds to find them homes. I felt sick as I looked at the photos of these animals, who through no fault of their own were going to die. This could easily have happened to George.

George had started to enjoy life and was giving back, so I thought, Why not? This is a chance for each of us to give back together, to help other dogs in need. I went back to the Surf City Surf Dog website, submitted my credit card number and registered George for the event. It was a great cause and we'd have fun. We would need to be in Huntington Beach at 8:00 a.m. on a Sunday to check in to the event. That was early, but I would deal with that then.

When that Sunday arrived, I groggily fumbled for the alarm clock to kill the annoying sound. As I struggled to open my eyes and regain consciousness, I felt a wet, sloppy tongue rub over my face like a big

brush at a car wash. The dog-surfing competition had seemed like a great idea when I'd registered weeks earlier, but at this sleep-deprived moment, it seemed like a horrible idea.

"Lie down, George," I muttered into my pillow. "We're going back to sleep."

Lick. Slobber. Wag.

I was determined to let sleep wash back over me, but George would have none of it. He made his intent known by sprawling across my back. Then, in case I hadn't noticed that, he gently nibbled on my ear, inhaling and exhaling right into my eardrum. I felt like I was in a wind tunnel. A loud, wet wind tunnel.

"George, seriously. Go lie down."

It was no use. As I lay there, I thought back to my grandfather's enthusiasm each morning at his cottage as he'd tell my brother and me about all the important things we had to do—swimming and building sand castles and flying kites—things worth getting out of bed for.

"Yeah, okay," I decided. "Let's go surfing. Let's do this, George." As soon as he saw me moving, his tail began to swish and his enthusiasm became contagious.

I got out of bed, threw on some board shorts and grabbed a hoodie and my flip-flops. I gathered our usual beach stuff in a bag, took George for a quick walk, fed him, then hooked him up to his leash and loaded him, our board and myself into the SUV. A quick stop at the Coffee Bean for the requisite early-morning latte and we hit the road, bound for Huntington Beach and our first encounter with the sport of dog surfing.

What am I doing? I thought as I sipped my coffee and headed down the highway with George in the back. Competitive dog surfing? I must be nuts.

By California standards it wasn't the nicest day. It was foggy and gray along the coast, and the waves, visible out the passenger window,

FREE DAYS WITH GEORGE

were bigger than usual. These waves would be tough even for experienced surfers. How in the world were dogs to stay on surfboards today?

I looked through the rearview mirror at George. He was sniffing excitedly at the open crack of the window, gulping in the moist ocean air. "This is going to be crazy, buddy. I need you to listen to me today. We're going to do something new." Like all the times I've ever spoken to George, I was saying things mostly for my own benefit, and wondered how much he understood, and yet I was always certain that he was listening.

We made it to Huntington Beach by 7:45, in time for the 8:00 a.m. check-in. I found a spot to park, opened the back door and let my big, galumphing dog jump out of the vehicle. Before walking down to the beach, we watched from afar and took in the crazy scene before us.

Huntington that Sunday was not the dog beach it normally was. Not in the least. It looked more like a carnival site and was filled with tents and exhibits, banners, foam surfboards, and hundreds of people and dogs of all shapes and sizes. Dogs were running around freely, playing and barking, while others were on leashes and stayed close by their owners' sides. The waves crashed on the beach, but the crackling walkie-talkies, the announcements from loudspeakers, the music playing in the background, the constantly chattering crowd and barking dogs matched the thunderous noise of the surf.

"Wow, this looks pretty crazy, George." We made our way down to the beach and were swallowed up in the circus atmosphere. There were bulldogs, pugs, retrievers and poodles. There was even a collie mix in a Superman costume, and a friendly pit bull with a plastic shark fin attached to his back. I couldn't get over the gear some of the dogs and owners had: surfboards emblazoned with dogs' names, and matching life jackets and custom-made T-shirts.

Then there was George and me. I was wearing rumpled clothes I'd salvaged from the floor, and George was dressed in nothing more than

his plain red collar. We made our way through chaos with our big, banged-up old board. "Excuse me, pardon me," I said, clearing a path through the sea of canines and owners all the way to the registration tent.

As we walked, I noticed out of the corner of my eye that people were stepping back to look at us. They were nudging each other and pointing at George in disbelief. Some shook their heads and others simply laughed and said, "Not a chance," or "No way." And that's when I realized that George was the largest dog at the competition—by far. He was a sumo wrestler in a room full of jockeys. It was also when I realized that no one in that crowd could believe George could surf.

We made our way to the end of the line at the registration tent and stood behind a guy with a rugged, round bulldog and a woman with a pug. After a few minutes it was our turn.

"Good morning," said a nice volunteer with dark hair and glasses. She was bent over the previous dog's registration papers so she hadn't yet looked up to see who was in front of her. When she did, George was staring at her at eye level.

"Whoa! That's one big dog. He's not . . . you're not— Is he *surfing* today?"

I didn't know what to say. For a second I felt like George and I were the awkward kids at school, the ones who are always picked last to be on the team. "Well," I finally managed, "he's going to try. Aren't you, George?"

George wagged his tail when he heard his name, leaned forward and kissed the woman's cheek.

She laughed and patted his head. "You're a big sweetie, aren't you? What kind of dog is he? He's huge!"

"He's a Newfoundland."

"Wow, he's the biggest dog we've ever had. I hope he knows how to surf."

"Oh, he should be okay," I said.

"Really?" She eyed me and then George.

"I think so," I said. "But we'll see how he does with all these people around. We're not really used to crowds."

"Okay, let's get him checked in." She shrugged, and then completed George's registration form. She explained that all the dogs were divided into different weight classes and that, not surprisingly, George was most definitely a heavyweight—dogs sixty pounds and up. Dogs and their handlers had ten minutes to catch as many waves as possible. A handler was allowed to help the dog onto the surfboard and get the surfboard positioned to catch the waves. The rest, like staying balanced and on the board, was up to the dog. George stared at her as she spoke, waiting for her to finish, and then planted a kiss on her the moment she paused.

"Oh, George, you're such a gentle giant," she said, as she looked back up at me. "Do you have any questions?"

"So he has to surf by himself? I'm not allowed on the board with him?"

"Yup. Those are the rules." I started to let that sink in, when she continued, "Most of the bigger dogs tend to jump off or lose their balance and fall because they're tall and have a high center of gravity. The short-legged breeds tend to do better. He might have some trouble."

George had never tried surfing by himself, and I had no idea if that would be a problem.

"Do you have a life jacket for him?" she asked, as she scratched George's ears.

"No," I said. "I never thought of bringing one. He's a very strong swimmer."

"Well, he's going to need a life jacket today," she said. "It's a liability issue. I just hope we have one big enough." She searched in a box of equipment and handed me the biggest life jacket she could find.

"Try it on him."

I was never inclined to dress George up in scarves or sweaters or fancy collars the way so many other dog owners did. It just didn't seem to suit him. So aside from his standard red collar, he'd never worn any kind of garment before. I adjusted the straps of the ratty bright-orange jacket to their maximum limit and clipped George in. The jacket wasn't nearly big enough. George looked like he was wearing a small child's hand-me-down. Still, the life jacket was on and it was not restricting his movement. She handed me a green competitor's scarf and I tied it around his neck to complete his dashing ensemble.

"What do you think, George?" He wagged his tail, gazed at me with excited eyes and jumped up to lick my face, resting his front paws on my shoulders and almost knocking me down. He was quite a sight: standing on his hind legs, he was nearly six feet tall, and wearing his tiny life jacket and green neck scarf—all told, he resembled an over-sized cartoon character. And he wasn't even on the surfboard yet.

"This is going to be interesting. Good luck, guys!" she said, and added, "You might need some."

"Thanks," I answered. "Come on, George." After a tug of the leash, George jumped back to all fours and we moved out of the line. As we did, a group of people nearby pulled out their cell phones and took pictures. George noticed the attention and immediately stretched out on his back in the sand, so that the whole crowd cooed "Aw-w-w-w-w" in unison and congregated around him to provide a mass belly rub.

I used that moment to process what the volunteer had just said: that George had to ride the board on his own. Whenever we'd surfed, it was always in tandem, George on the front of the board and me kneeling on the back. I had no idea if he could or would surf on his own. A sense of uneasiness set in. Had I just set George up for failure by entering him in a competition to do something he couldn't do? And

what was I supposed to do when we were out there in front of all those people and cameras if George couldn't get on the board? And if he did get on the board, what if he didn't want to surf without me?

All these questions made me feel queasy, but when I looked down at the sand in front of me and saw George sprawled out, oblivious to my concern, soaking up all the love of his new admirers, I realized I was over-thinking the matter. This was, after all, just a fun event to raise money for dogs—dogs needing homes. If George was happy in the midst of the crowd, I could be, too. I was ready to help him get on the surfboard, but if for some reason he didn't want to, that was fine. The money would still go to a good cause.

With George fully registered and equipped, we headed back to the SUV to get our towels, sunscreen, water, bowls, umbrella and other odds and ends. I set up our umbrella in a nice, quiet spot away from the Surf Dog judges' tent. "Let's just sit here a minute, George," I said, and he plopped his rear end next to me. Together we took in the sights and sounds around us.

I'm convinced that such a crazy event has never been seen anywhere outside Southern California. The crowd was definitely growing as the start time neared. There were even more dogs in costume now, some wearing sunglasses and some sporting custom-made board shorts that matched the ones worn by their owners. The Beach Boys echoed over the loudspeakers, and many owners had already donned their wet suits, preparing to take their family pets into the water to compete. The coconut smell of sunscreen blended with that unmistakable *eau de wet dog* perfume. It was an olfactory experience like nothing else.

The number of volunteers seemed to have doubled in the forty-five minutes we'd been at the beach and the vendor booths set up in rows on the sand were now hawking everything from dog food, to dog

toys, to dog collars and every other kind of dog-related paraphernalia under the sun. George was getting more and more excited, prancing on his front paws in that way of his that meant, "Let me loose!"

"You need to behave, big guy." George eyed me with a look that said, "I have no idea what you're talking about, but you gotta let me go play."

"Okay, George, go have fun," I said, unclipping him from the leash. He gave me one big lick and then ran down to the water, followed by a pack of other dogs wearing life jackets that actually fit. It was one of the strangest sights I have ever seen. Evidently I wasn't the only one to notice the oddity, because soon enough a group of photographers was taking pictures of the ragtag pack running in circles and jumping in and out of the water.

I overheard an older couple on a nearby blanket: "See that big black-and-white dog over there?" She was pointing at George.

"Yeah," her husband answered.

"He's going to be surfing today."

"No way! I can't *wait* to see that!"

"George!" I called out after a few minutes of watching him play with his new friends. "Come here!" His big head went up, and he trotted over to me, looking waterlogged but happy with himself in his ridiculously tiny life jacket and wet neck scarf.

"Good boy, George," I said as he walked right under the umbrella, following my instructions on the first command. He barreled into me and shook his coat, sending spray and sand everywhere and eliciting an audible chorus of shrieks and laughter from the other beach umbrellas in our midst. George was basking in the attention and excitement, glancing all around him and practically smiling from head to toe. I thought back to nine months earlier and the terrified dog in my dining room, too frightened to even move on his own. He was

hardly recognizable as the same dog. It was an incredible transformation, and for a moment I was overcome by a feeling of pride.

"Here, big guy," I said. "Have a drink." I offered him his water bowl. As George splashed his water about, getting more on our blanket than into his mouth, a thin brunette with a huge smile walked over to us and peeked under our umbrella.

"Hi, I'm Lisa Scolman," she said. "I'm one of the organizers of the event." She extended a hand and I shook it.

"I'm Colin," I replied. Then, nodding at my sloppy, wet dog, I added, "And this is George."

"Hello, George!" she said. "Some of the staff told me a 'super-huge' dog had entered. I wanted to meet him for myself."

George took to Lisa right away, pushing his full wet weight into her and craning his neck to look her in the eye.

She laughed. "They weren't kidding. You really are a big boy, aren't you?"

She bent to pet him, and George rolled over on his shoulder and then onto his back, showing her his belly, which was covered in sand.

"Someone's already been swimming." She rubbed his belly, not the least bit concerned with getting wet or sandy herself. "So he's really surfed before?"

"Yes," I said. "We have surfed together a bit, haven't we, George?"

She shook her head, amazed. "I just can't even imagine. Most of the dogs we see in the competition have a low center of gravity, but George . . . well, he's got those long legs, and he's just so . . . big. So, are you going to get up on a board today, George?"

I was wondering the same thing myself.

"If nothing else, he'll add his big personality to the event," she said.

She had stopped petting George as she spoke, and he now put a large, wet paw on her arm as a subtle reminder that she was neglecting

her belly-rubbing duty. "You sure are something, George," she said. "I'm so glad you came out with him. It's a fun event, and we raise a lot of money for rescue dogs."

"That's why we entered. He was a homeless dog, too," I said. "He's come a long way."

Looking me right in the eye, she said, "You're really lucky to have him." And as I stood there watching George lying on his back on the beach, getting his belly rubbed by a friendly stranger on the edge of the Pacific Ocean, that's when it struck me: you never do know where life will take you if you let it. This once-terrified and neglected dog from Canada was now in California and about to go surfing in a crazy dog-surfing contest. He really had come far, literally and figuratively.

So what about me? How had I ended up here? A year and a half earlier, I'd suffered the biggest loss of my life. And now I'd been transplanted from everything I once knew to this beach, in another country so far away from my home. When I was completely alone, this dog had become my good friend. He got me up in the morning. He made me laugh, forced me to take walks and meet new people. He even brought me to the beach, where we discovered by accident the one thing we both so loved to do: surf. It suddenly hit me with profound force: I had rescued George, but really, it was he who was rescuing me.

Getting George's life jacket on at the Surf City Surf Dog Competition in 2010.

George nibbling at my ear.

George meeting some well-dressed surfing dogs in the small division in the Surf City Surf Dog competition in 2010.

George was always a favorite of the "puparazzi" whenever he was at the beach.

George in early takeoff, catching a wave. That's me and a volunteer just above the crest of the wave.

George carving it up.

George enjoying a post-championship drink at a Mexican restaurant in Huntington Beach.

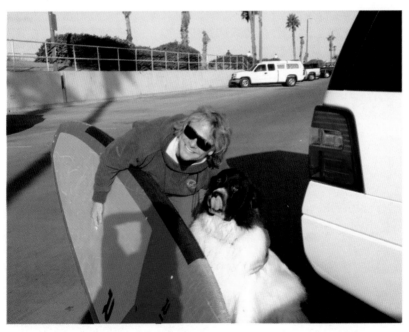

A few years later, George and I arrive at Huntington Beach for the 2014 Surf City Surf Dog competition.

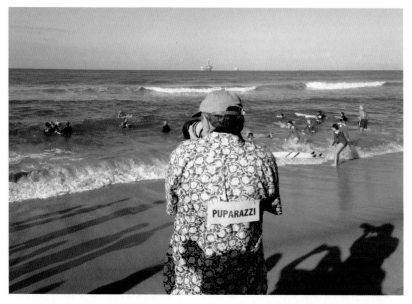

As usual, the camera crews and "puparazzi" record all the action as the small dogs begin their heat.

George and I relax in the sand before we get ready to hit the waves.

Here, we sit on the shore and rest after George let me know that he'd had enough for one day.

© Suzanne Haggerty

George was a much older dog when he entered the competition in 2014. With age comes wisdom, which you can see on George's face.

A few days after the 2014 competition, George and I went out surfing on our own and had a "free day" together at the Newport Beach jetty.

Another fabulous ride at Newport, 2014. Who said old dogs can't do new tricks?

Ever the lifeguard, George gently leads me by the hand out of the water to safety.

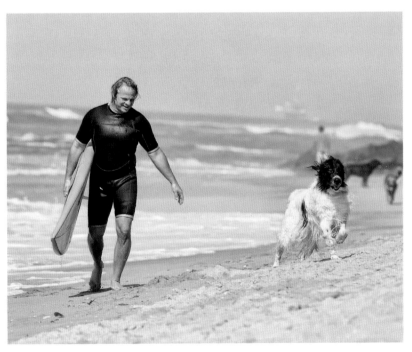

There's nothing like a good run and shake after a perfect day of surfing.

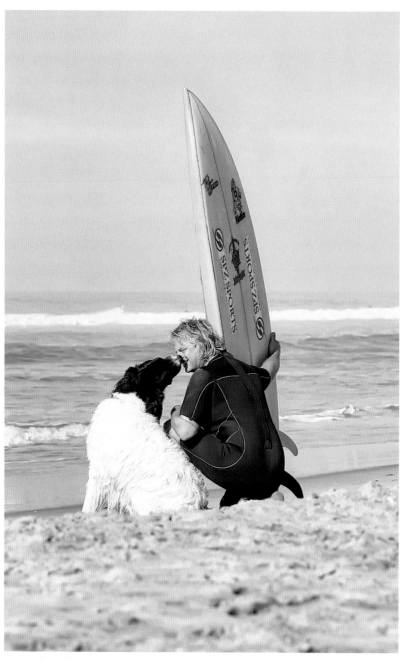

One of my favorite pictures—it totally sums up our "free days" at the beach together.

George always makes sure that I'm all right when we swim together.
Nova Scotia, 2014.

George having a nap on the couch in 2014—proof that he can make himself comfortable anywhere. It's too bad the photo can't convey the snoring.

While George is a very large Newfoundland, he thinks he's a Chihuahua.

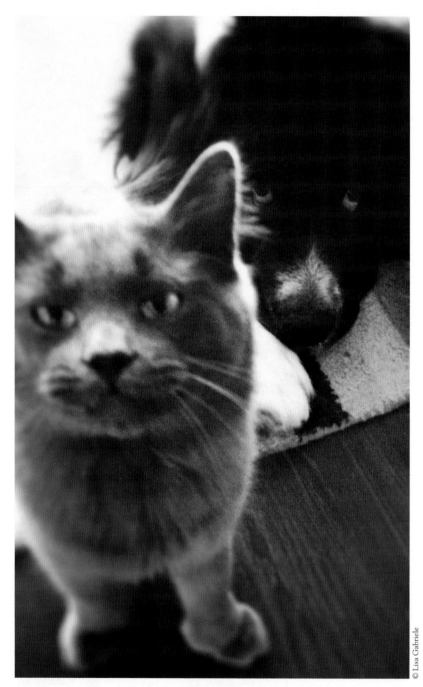

George and his buddy Charlie, the very best of friends.

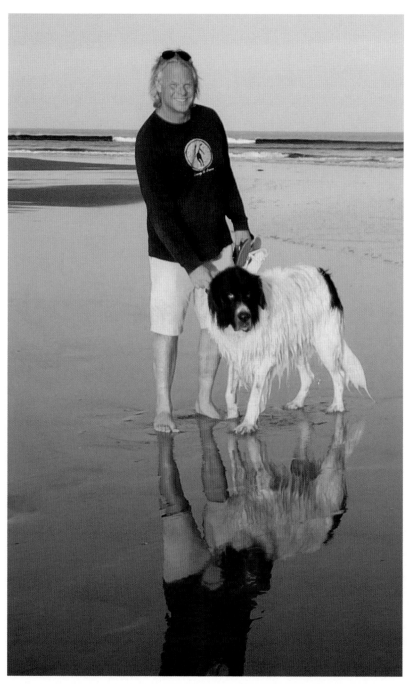

Enjoying the setting sun at Cherry Hill Beach in Nova Scotia.

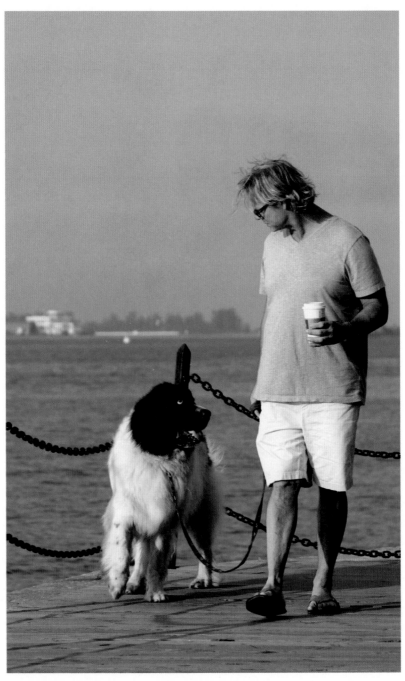

Walking together on the waterfront in Toronto, 2014.

EIGHTEEN

J ust then the music stopped and the PA system announced that the first heat of small dogs was taking to the water. "Oops," Lisa said. "I've got to run. It was so good to meet you. Hope you ride a wave as big as you, George!" she said. "Nice meeting you both."

"Very nice meeting you, too," I said. She tore off to the judges' tent, and George and I settled in to watch the first heat.

The Beach Boys faded out and an announcer said, "Good morning, dog lovers and surf lovers! Welcome to the Surf City Surf Dog competition! We're thrilled to have you here today, and we're about to get started with the first heat of small dogs—up to twenty pounds. But small is no barrier when it comes to surfing, so you're about to see some pretty amazing canine carving, folks!"

The judges, three well-respected pro surfers, took their positions in a high stand on the beach. The crowd moved closer to the water's edge. Several reporters ran by George and me on the beach on their way to get a better view. I knew they were with the media not just because of their nice cameras with large lenses but because of identifying signs pinned to their backs: PUPARAZZI.

The competition was in many ways just like a real pro surfing

event, except instead of Kelly Slater, Brett Simpson or Taj Burrow, these surfers had names like Hanzo, Ricochet and Dozer.

"And taking to the beach are today's minute-but-mighty contestants . . ." Their owners brought the competing dogs to the shoreline and turned to wave at the crowd. Once they were all in a row, the announcer said, "And those are your small surfers, ladies and gentlemen, just about ready to take the waves!"

The crowd started to clap and cheer, and from where George and I were seated we could see owners doing last checks of life jackets and giving encouraging pats to their dogs.

Pugs were very well represented in the first heat, their wide stance and low center of gravity offering a natural advantage, but the talent pool ran the gamut from Chihuahuas to Boston terriers. All of them were decked out in life jackets and colored scarves to help the judges recognize them—their gear was nice and new and fit well, unlike George's last-minute outfit, I noted once again.

All along the lineup, owners picked up their pets as though they were dog-shaped briefcases, and when the air horn sounded, off they ran—dogs in one hand, boards in the other—splashing into the ocean. Because these dogs were so small, they didn't go out past the break. Instead they focused on riding the smaller waves in the white water close to shore. It was hilarious watching the handlers position their animals on their mini boards and struggle to keep the boards still until the moment they let go. Then each dog would either ride the wave victoriously to shore as people cheered and hollered the dog's name, or the little surfer got knocked off the board and the crowd let out a unified gasp of dismay. The crowd would resume cheering as soon as the little dog appeared in the foam, doggie-paddling madly back to the board. "Go, girl, go! You can do it this time! Get back on there!"

I was surprised when I found myself as caught up in the event as

everyone else at the beach, and when an incredible little dog named Bobby ably surfed wave after wave after wave, I found myself on my feet, clapping right alongside everyone else. Meanwhile, cameras were going off everywhere and volunteers on the shore were scrambling to grab stray surfboards. In all directions there was mass pandemonium for the full duration of the heat. It was totally fun.

I held on to George's life jacket while I was watching, and at one point I turned to look at him. "What do you think, George?"

He was focused on the beach and seemed to be studying the water. There one of the dogs he had been playing with earlier took to the board on a smooth, spectacular ride. George spotted him and did his signature two-step puppy hopping on his back legs to get a better view. "Pretty cool, isn't it, George?" I said. I, too, tried to observe, so I could see how owners were helping their dogs get on the boards, but from the shoreline it was hard to make out any consistent techniques. Owners seemed to have their own methods for helping their dogs hop on. A couple of the dogs appeared a little frightened, but for the most part it was clear these were animals who loved to surf and didn't mind very much when the waves got the better of them, tossing them into the ocean; they would swim back out for another try.

After ten minutes the air horn blew, and the competitors and handlers made their way to shore. I had to laugh as a couple of the dogs needed to be put on leashes because they wanted to stay out for more.

"And that's the end of the first heat, everyone! We had a great set out there for our first run. We saw shredders and floaters and a couple of really impressive wipeouts, too. Way to go, little guys! Miniature can be mighty! Give it up for the dogs!"

A huge whoop issued from the crowd. "Our judges will soon post competitors who will move on to our finals round this afternoon, but in the meantime, let's get ready for our medium-sized-dog heats—for

dogs twenty-one to forty pounds. All competitors please make your way to the judges' tent."

The heats continued in this fashion from small to medium to large, and even though I was starting to feel a bit tired, the crowd, the dogs and their owners were, if anything, getting more excited. In between heats George received a steady stream of visitors. Most couldn't believe he was actually a competitor and had stopped by just to see the big dog and confirm the rumor for themselves.

The sheer volume of people who wanted to meet George was unlike anything I'd ever seen. He was like a rock star or royalty. He was meeting a new person every thirty seconds. As he had been on so many of our previous outings and adventures, George was hugged and petted over and over. He posed for pictures and he gave out kisses freely. He was far more comfortable and confident than I had ever seen him, even with men. And he didn't get tired of the attention; in fact, he seemed energized by it. He had been off his leash most of the morning and had never strayed too far from me. Whenever he wandered off to meet new people or dogs, he would stop after a minute or so and check over his shoulder to make sure he could still see me. I could not have trained him to behave this well if I had tried. And I had.

"Is that your dog over there?" I was asked repeatedly.

"Yep. He's mine."

As they always seemed to, the repetitive questions and answers about my big black-and-white dog went on and on and on:

"What kind of dog is he?" "A Newfoundland."

"How much does he weigh?" "One hundred forty pounds."

"Does he eat a lot?" "Surprisingly, not really."

"And he's really going to surf?" "I hope so."

"And he's done it before?" "He has. He loves it."

"What's his name?" "George."

FREE DAYS WITH GEORGE

"Aw-w-w-w-w. George! Can I pet him?" "You sure can. He'd like that."

Finally, the loudspeakers announced more news. "Okay, folks. Now we're ready for our last round of competitors. It's time for the heavyweights, the extra-large division! Please make your way down to the water."

"Okay, George. We're up," I said. I excused George from his current set of fans, put on my wet suit and gave George another drink of water. "Let's go."

He wagged his tail as hard as he had all day. I picked up our surfboard and we walked over to the epicenter of the competition—the judges' tent. I looked down at George as he cut through the crowd like a boxer entering the ring. People had their phones and cameras out, taking pictures and pointing. "There he is! That's the big dog I was telling you about!" Or, "Good luck, George!"

He had his chest puffed out and was turning his head from side to side, acknowledging everyone who was watching him. He looked every person in the eye. Once we arrived at the tent, I bent and whispered in his ear, "Are you ready?" I was still a bit unsure of what we were about to do, but he seemed ready to go.

In front of us was a retriever with its owner, who was carrying a custom surfboard with the dog's name written across it. At the judges' area, a goldendoodle was sitting with her people, including a film crew who were documenting her experience. Obviously this was the competitor to watch. George and I—my Newf with his tiny, poorly fitting life jacket and me carrying the most beat-up surfboard at the beach— looked like we didn't know what we were doing. The appearance wasn't deceiving. Going up against dogs owning brand-new surfboards and having their own videographers made me feel a bit underprepared. It was like the moment in every Disney sports movie when the heroic underdogs see their much slicker, better-funded nemesis. But George

didn't care at all about the other dogs' equipment and I liked that. I followed his lead and just focused on us.

We arrived at the water's edge and took a place a ways off from the other competitors. Among the dogs in George's heat were two retrievers, a German shepherd, an enormous bulldog and the goldendoodle. One retriever was jumping around in a mad rush of excitement and the other was having a hard time staying awake. The brick-shaped bulldog was standing beside his spanking-new blue-and-gray surfboard. The goldendoodle reclined in the sand as though modeling for a swimsuit calendar. Her film crew huddled around her, recording her every move.

As for the handlers, they varied as much as the dogs. The owner of the bulldog greeted me and George in a friendly, relaxed way. One of the owners of the labs was very excited and raring to go, circling his dog and checking his equipment. As I took in this scene, I became aware of just how big George was. He was the biggest dog by at least fifty pounds. It was also the first moment of the day that no one paid us attention. It was kind of nice to focus on each other rather than on the carnival around us.

One of the judges approached and explained some of the rules. "Remember, the goal is to catch as many waves as you can in ten minutes, and we award extra points for tricks."

The owners around us nodded. They all knew the drill, but we didn't.

"Tricks?" I asked.

"Yeah. Like riding backward. Or walking up to the nose of the surfboard. That kinda thing."

I was just hoping George would get on the board and not fall off!

"The contest begins in just a couple of minutes. If you can please lay out your boards in the sand and wait till you hear the air horn blow. That's your signal to take to the waves with your pooches. And good luck!" The judge scampered back to his post at the judges' stand, and I positioned our giant board at the edge of the shore as instructed.

George followed and immediately stood on it, proud as a peacock. I could hear people laughing and cameras clicking away. So much for our quiet moment out of the spotlight.

I dropped to one knee on the sand beside George and put my hand on the back of his head. He was calm, alert, and he seemed as happy as ever, looking at me as if asking, "So what's next?"

"Let's go have fun," I said, giving his head a nuzzle. He returned the affection in his big, sloppy way.

The clouds had blown over somewhat and the sun was shining through small breaks in the sky. The waves hadn't diminished in the slightest, and in fact were getting larger. The other dogs and owners were in a line down the beach, watching the water, as was George.

The shrill blast of the air horn pierced the air and was echoed by the cheering crowd. "Let's go!" I shouted, and George ran beside me, matching me stride for stride, into the rolling surf. I dived across the surface with the board underneath me and started to paddle out. Out of the corner of my eye, I could see the other handlers getting in the water and their dogs swimming out to sea beside them.

George stayed close by my side, and his powerful stroke allowed us to reach the break well before anyone else. Getting past the break and into the open ocean is the hardest part of surfing, whether amateur or pro, human or dog. Human surfers usually dive under the waves then surface on the other side of them and continue to paddle out, a physically demanding technique. With most dogs, however, diving under is ruled out by their instinct to keep their head above water. Not so George—he would go under a wave without a second thought. The hard part was what to do with him once he surfaced, how to help him onto the board in these massive waves, the likes of which we'd never seen. Getting him balanced on the board was like trying to set a table inside a working washing machine.

I jumped off the surfboard into chest-deep water, with George swimming powerfully a few feet beside me. A wall of white water rolled in, and I pushed the nose of the surfboard down to allow the water to wash over it. As I did this, I kept my eye on George, who had instinctively ducked his head into the wave and kept his legs churning forward. The wall of water washed over both of us and his head popped up to the surface two seconds later—he had been pushed back only a couple feet. I couldn't have trained him to do it any better. "Whew! Good boy, George!" I yelled over the sound of the waves crashing around us.

He churned toward me and in a matter of seconds had his two front paws up on the surfboard. Newfoundlands are legendary for their bravery and strength in the ocean, and today the instincts of George's breed were coming into good use. I took his webbed paws in my hands as he looked me in the eye with an intensity I had never seen in him. Half out of breath, I said, "I'm going to push your bum up on the board, and you're going to *stay*. Okay?" I knew he wouldn't understand, but I also knew my tone would keep him focused and that he did understand the most important word I'd said: *stay*.

We had about ten more seconds before the next wall of white water would roll over top of us. I grabbed one his back legs and pushed his rear end up onto the board. And just like that, he was on the board by himself. "*Stay*, George!" He stood steady as a statue. His long legs, which I'd been warned were a liability, were actually an asset when getting through the break because the waves were flowing between his body and the partially submerged board. I pulled the board beside me and lay down on the back, paddling us forward as hard as I could. One more wave and we'd clear the break and be in the right place to turn around and catch a wave in.

The big wave was almost upon us. "Hang tight, George. *Stay*." If we didn't time it right, it would crash right on top of us. The front of the board rose and we almost got to forty-five degrees as the wave

peaked. We fell forward quickly as the wave surged underneath us, but George kept his balance and did not move. We made it past the break! I looked back to see most of our competitors still behind us, getting dunked while trying to swim over the breaking waves.

Even with a bit of a head start, life past the break was intimidating. The waves were up to seven feet high, which was the upper limit of anything I had ever tried to surf by myself, never mind with George. Safe from breaking waves for a moment, I caught my breath and started to map out our next step. Basically I had to turn the board around and get George's weight centered so he could surf by himself. If he was too far forward, as soon as the wave started moving George would be catapulted into the water in a huge wipeout. If he was too far back, the wave would wash underneath him and he would go nowhere.

All George wanted to do was lick my face. He turned around and plastered me with kisses. "George, cut it out for a second. There are hundreds of people watching." Treading water beside the board, I had to move his legs to get him properly positioned. He thought this was a fun game and he kept moving back to his previous spot on the board. After a few tries, when he was finally dead center and in the proper position, I told him to sit. And he did.

"Good boy! Stay, George," I said. Then I spun the board around so it pointed toward the shore. "We are waiting for a good wave and you are going to surf back into the beach like a pro."

I looked behind us and saw a big six-footer heading our way. It was a perfectly formed California wave—a smooth, legendary wall of water, the kind surfers from around the world come to test their skills on. "Here we go," I said as calmly as possible.

I pushed the surfboard in sync with the wave and let go . . . and it worked. It totally worked! For a few glorious seconds the wave picked up the board and sped George toward the shore. *He was surfing by himself!*

He sat perfectly, head high. I was ecstatic. I could hear the roar of the crowd! He surfed past one of the retrievers struggling to find its board. Then, after a few more seconds, he stirred and looked over his shoulder. The question was written on his face plain as day: "Where is he?" George then turned himself around completely, surfing backward as he spotted me in the water.

I saw his big eyes open wide. Oh no. He's going to come back for me. And a second later George dived off the board. The spectators groaned. He swam back through the surf toward me. When he reached me, he took my forearm in his mouth and started to pull me to the safety of the beach.

When we arrived, I stood up. "See?" I told him. "I'm fine."

A volunteer grabbed our surfboard, and when George saw it, he began wagging his tail.

A few spectators yelled, "Good boy, George! That was amazing!" and "Try it again!" George glanced at them, head cocked. He didn't think surfing a big wave was anything special at all. He gazed up at me as if to ask, "What's next?"

I retrieved the surfboard, and George began to prance on the shoreline, ready to go back out. I looked out at the break and was pleased to see some of the other dogs getting short rides in. "Let's go again, George!" I said.

This time he hopped on the board early, and I guided him straight to the break. He managed to keep his balance as we made it through the white water. George had started to catch on to the positioning part and now sat balanced in the middle of the board. Convincing him to stay on the board by himself, though, proved to be a problem. A big problem. On our next three attempts he was perfectly placed for big waves, but every time I released the board, within a second or two he'd turn around and see me in the water behind him. He had that look on

his face that said, "Hold on, I'm coming to save you!" Then he'd jump off the moving surfboard and swim back to me.

The fourth attempt, though, with time about to run out, I released him onto the face of a wave that was tall enough to hide me in its trough. When I could see him again, he was peering around for me, but he'd already stayed in place longer than on any previous run. The wave broke and the white water continued to take him to shore when he finally spotted me—he'd managed to turn in a run lasting a full eight seconds! People on the beach cheered and I was speechless.

Eventually George casually jumped off the board, and instead of heading to shore the way the other dogs did, he did a quick U-turn in the shallow water and swam out to "save" me yet again. I met him in chest-deep water and this time he put his paws up on my shoulders. I gave him a big hug as he licked my face. The air horn sounded—the ten minutes had gone by fast. We made our way out of the water just as the stocky bulldog took a nice, final wave. The retrievers and the goldendoodle were shaking themselves off and wagging their tails, glad to be back on shore.

"Let's hear it for the extra-large dogs!" the announcer said. "They were fearless canines out there, taking the tallest waves of the day, and we saw some amazing rides from one very big Newfoundland, some great retrievers and from one very solid bulldog, too! Well done!"

I really had no idea how George had done compared to the other dogs in the heat, but the crowd seemed thrilled with his performance and a few people were chanting his name. The surfing was hard, unlike anything we had ever done, but George had clearly had fun.

Just then a group of photographers, all carrying telephoto lenses, asked to take our picture.

"That was incredible," one photographer said. "Never seen anything like it."

It felt very strange, like George and I had gone from not really fitting in to becoming celebrities in a matter of minutes. George, still wearing his goofy life jacket, was soaked to the skin and covered in sand. Nevertheless he posed as if he had been doing it all his life—head up, chest out and legs set wide and strong, like a duke's prized hound in an English oil painting.

Then without warning he shook himself off, spectacularly soaking the photographers and spectators, eliciting shrieks and a huge burst of laughter. "Nice one, George. Thanks!" one of the photographers said. Upon hearing his name, George looked at him as if to say, "What, did I do something wrong?"

"George, you're a piece of work."

A couple of kids wandered over. "Can we hug him?" they asked me. "He was so good out there. He's my favorite dog!"

"Sure you can hug him—if you don't mind getting wet." The kids pounced on George, giving him huge hugs that were returned with big, sloppy dog kisses. The photographers captured it all on camera—George's loving personality shining as brightly as I had ever seen. He was happy, beyond happy. He was at peace and at home. And for the first time since I could remember, I felt the same way.

The photographers got what they needed and drifted off, but the attention George received didn't waver. I took him back to our umbrella and blanket, removed his life jacket and neck scarf, intending to let him rest, but it was impossible—there were just too many people who wanted to meet him.

The owner of the bulldog from our heat came over. "I saw you guys getting through that break—congrats! You must be looking forward to doing it again in the finals this afternoon."

"Finals?" I didn't think being in the finals was something George and I needed to worry about.

"Yeah. Bruno and I made it through and so did you and George. It's going to be fun!"

I was shocked. "I had no clue George did that well. I guess we'll see you out there again later."

"For sure! Can't wait. And good luck!"

"Thanks. Same to you!"

After he left, a crowd formed in front of our umbrella, and George provided hugs, kisses and photo ops for everyone who stopped by. If he could have signed autographs, he would have done that, too. After twenty minutes or so, the crowd went away and George, still wet and covered in sand, flaked out on the blanket and promptly started snoring.

Poor George was worn out. He'd already had quite the day. And while I knew he had enjoyed every minute—as had I—I also knew he wasn't used to surfing twice in one day. Looking down at the big, tired dog, still rumbling and fast asleep, I decided that I would let George choose if he wanted to go out there again. I was learning by then that the leash between us worked two ways and that sometimes it was important to follow his lead. If George woke up with renewed energy and wanted to surf in the finals, he would. And if he didn't, that was fine with me, too.

George was still sleeping an hour later when the announcer took to the loudspeaker once more to say that the finals were about to begin. George opened one eye, then the other. He looked around and hopped to his feet as if he couldn't believe he'd missed any of the action. "Good nap, George?" I asked, and he flapped his ears, shaking the

sleep off. I gave him some of his favorite cookies and a fresh bowl of water, which he lapped up eagerly.

When he was finished, I asked, "You ready to go back out there? Totally up to you." I got up and began gathering the surfboard and his life jacket, watching George for clues. His tail started wagging when he saw the surfboard under my arm. He arched his back and stretched his legs in a perfect downward dog pose.

"Want to put this back on?" I asked, as I grabbed his life jacket. He pushed his head into the hole and waited for me to fasten the clips. "Good boy!"

Once the mini life jacket was on, I led him over to the starting area. Decked out for competition yet again, he walked with a bit of a strut, but this time as he parted the crowd, he didn't turn to the people who called his name. There was a new determination in him, as if he were saying, "Let's get this show on the road."

We gathered on the sand with the other dogs in the heavyweight final. The crowd had grown larger and there were now not just hundreds of people on the beach but well over a thousand. The competition area was roped off and the announcer was amping up the crowd:

"Let's welcome back Shad, Bruno, the brash and brave bulldog . . . and weighing in at a *lo-o-o-t* of pounds, the biggest dog ever to grace a board in this competition, the friendly Newfoundland . . . George!"

The cheer from the crowd went up louder than I expected. Some kids started to chant, "George! George! George! George!" He turned his head to watch them and wagged his tail. Everyone started to laugh, and I couldn't help but smile. It felt great to know that George was a catalyst for a lot of the smiles and joy on that beach. In the morning I'd felt a bit unsure about what we were doing, even though George was, as usual, ten paces ahead of me and happy just to be alive. But

now, taking in the warmth from the California sun and from the smiles of the people gathered there, I was feeling the joy, too.

Moments later the air horn sounded, and off we went into the surf, dogs and owners and boards. We were running and laughing as we made our way to the water. The waves were still big, and I held the board down against them. George jumped on before we even made it out. "Want a ride?" I asked as I paddled him out to the first wall of white water. The front of the board went high up into the air, but we managed to make it over and I kept paddling as hard as I could. The next wave, however, was far closer than the others had been in the morning, and before I knew it, we were in "no man's land"—a place so close to the wave that we couldn't turn around or keep paddling forward because it was going to break right on top of us.

"Hang on, George!" I yelled as a cascade of greenish-blue water dropped almost directly on our heads. The board went spiraling skyward dramatically, and George and I were pummeled and submerged. I knew to hold my breath, to relax until the chaos of the wave washed by, but did George? After a few long seconds I rolled to the surface and cleared my eyes of water, searching for him. He wasn't there. Oh no, I thought, but the next thing I saw was his head popping out of the water about six feet behind me.

"George!" He turned toward me and started swimming as fast as he could. "It's okay, big guy. I'm all right." But he was determined to grab my arm and tow me back to shore. "You're a good boy, George," I said as I gave in, wrapping my arms around his neck and letting him take me to shallow water. Bruno the Bulldog surfed right past us as the crowd cheered.

Back on the shore, the volunteers ran over to us with George's board. They were breathless. "There's still time! Take him out again!" I could hear a few people in the crowd chanting George's name, and so

could he. I crouched next to George on the sand. "Up to you, big guy. Want to try again?" I went to grab the board, and George hopped back on in the shallow water and we started to paddle our way out.

A few minutes later we made it past the break without falling. I got George in position. He was becoming used to this game. "Okay, George, sit . . . *stay.* Good boy." I went to the back of the board to push, but he was trying to turn around to check on me, which was throwing his balance off. Just as the next swell rose behind us, I pushed the board as hard as I could, but instead of going straight, because he had his weight on the left side of the board it headed about forty degrees to the left, along the face of the wave. It was actually the best way for human surfers to take off, but it wasn't ideal for dogs, who need to be square to the wave for better stability. For a few seconds he couldn't see me behind the cresting wave and he stayed focused and balanced on the board. As soon as the wave broke, however, he tumbled off in a spectacular wipeout.

The whole ride lasted only a few seconds, but it was a quality ride. I was later told that from shore this ride looked amazing. This time, instead of swimming back for me, George ran to the beach. I swam to shore to meet him where he was sitting, wagging his tail, tongue out. I plopped down beside him and he put a big, wet paw on my leg. "You're tired. Let's catch our breath, big guy," I said. There was no urgency about anything. We sat like that, side by side on the beach, with the crowd chanting and cheering behind us, and watched the other incredible dogs still out catching their waves.

A few minutes later I noticed our surfboard was caught in the backwash and was drifting out toward the surf. I jumped up to grab it and haul it to shore, but as I did, George jumped up, too, and ran right by me into the water and climbed onto the board. By the time I caught up to him, the air horn sounded. The finals were over, and fittingly, George was standing proudly on his beat-up rental board. He had not

been the best surfing dog in the finals, but there was no denying he was the biggest and happiest dog on the beach. I was so proud of him. If I'd had a tail, I would have been wagging it, too.

An awards ceremony was to follow on the beach, and after George and I cleaned up a bit, we went down to watch. The organizers had brought out a podium and were awarding surfboard-shaped medals to the day's winners.

It was quite a sight to see, as handlers and dogs made their way to the podium and the dogs, despite being tired from a full day of activity at the ocean, perked right up as soon as they were in front of the crowd. Owners spoke on behalf of their pets, often praising the organizers for hosting the event and for doing such a good job of raising money for rescue dogs, a cause close to everyone's heart.

George and I were standing at the back of the crowd when the winners for the extra-large division were called up. One of the retrievers was declared the winner and Bruno the Bulldog came second—and to my surprise, George got third. "Wow, George, you came in third!" I said. We made our way through the crowd, with people clapping, some reaching out to pat George and some reaching out to shake my hand.

When we reached the podium, Lisa gave me a hug and tried to place a surfing medal around George's neck. Of course it was too small, which elicited laughter from the crowd. As we were making our way back through the crowd to our spot at the rear, I heard, "Ladies and gentlemen, all our winners have been announced, so now it's time to call upon the dog that you chose as a favorite. It's time to hand out the People's Choice Award for Crowd Pleaser! George, don't walk away so soon. Will you please come to the podium again."

I was pretty sure I'd heard wrong.

"They're calling you," some fellow dog owners said to George and me.

"Wow, really?" We moved back through the crowd, receiving more pats and handshakes, and when we made it to the front, there was Lisa again, smiling from ear to ear.

"Congratulations to George, and to you, too, Colin. We're so happy that you joined us today. I know everyone was excited to have not only such a big dog out surfing today, but such a sweet dog with a bigger personality. I'm so pleased to be giving George this special medal for winning the Crowd Pleaser Award."

Lisa crouched in front of George and tucked the second medal into his collar, as another peal of laughter issued from the crowd. He thanked her with one of his big, sloppy kisses. A volunteer handed us a large prize bag of dog stuff—leashes, toys, collars, bowls, treats and dog food. George put his head into the bag and sniffed, but he was definitely more interested in the people around him than the treats. He then threw his head back, gave a small howl and did a shoulder roll onto his back, where he received a champion's belly rub.

Once the ceremonies were over, the judges came over and shook my hand. "He's really quite something, your dog," they said. "We've never seen any dog like him."

I was so proud of him. "Thanks," I said. "Did you hear that, George?"

George turned to look up at us, a giant "Huh?" written all over his face. I got down to his level and wrapped him in an enormous hug. George getting an award not for his surfing but for being an all-around nice dog and for spreading smiles and love was the unexpected perfect ending to a perfect day.

Once the awards ceremony was over, I thought George and I would head home and spend a quiet evening relaxing . . . but not before being approached by more spectators, competitors and volunteers—dozens of people, all offering their congratulations.

"You're so lucky. He's a beautiful dog." I had never heard it so often and with such conviction. This time, the full weight of it struck me. *I really am lucky.*

Nine months earlier George had been so emotionally broken that any contact with a stranger or any sudden movement would make him very afraid. Twenty months earlier I, too, had suffered a big emotional loss and a change that made me back away from life. I realized on that day just how much disappointment and sadness about the breakup of my marriage I'd still been holding on to. I'd been closing myself off from people and experiences in my personal life, and I was failing to recognize and embrace all that life offers, especially in someplace as nice as Southern California. How could I take so much for granted and be going through the motions of life in such a daze? George lived brightly and beautifully—every day. He'd given back a thousand times over whatever love I'd sent his way, and he graciously offered love to anyone who offered it to him. He was happy and grateful every day.

In that moment I felt myself let go of all the pain. Instead of defining my existence through the loss of my marriage, I looked at George and saw how to define myself through love, friendship and joy. I had someone who loved me as deeply as anyone ever had. And I was happy—I had every reason to be.

The saying "A dog is a man's best friend" isn't a cliché for me; it's a lived experience. It's an acknowledgment that life's best gifts can come at

any time, even when we least expect them. They can come in some very large packages, too, some even wrapped in fur and slobbery kisses.

After the excitement and upheaval of the contest, George and I finally did get our quiet night at home. We packed up all our gear and headed up the Pacific Coast Highway to Bruce Jones's Surf Shop, where we rinsed off all the saltwater and sand.

We drove home, ate some dinner and went for a walk. It was a normal night. George still had to do his business—his *big* business—and I still had to pick it up. We watched a little TV, George snoozing at my feet, and I eventually went to bed and read for a while. After a few minutes George lumbered over and hopped up in bed beside me. I put down my book and gave his big, velvety ears a rub. The love I felt for him was bursting through my heart and I couldn't tell him enough.

I had a vivid flash of memory back to when I was a kid and my brother and I were tucked in our bunk beds at my grandfather's cottage after a full day of sun and play. I saw my grandfather in a chair beside us, finishing the last page of the bedtime story we'd asked him to read:

"Boys, we had a pretty good day today, didn't we?"

Of course we did. With Grandpa we always did.

"Boys, when you're lucky enough to spend a day with someone you love, doing things you enjoy, you don't grow old that day. Today was a free day on earth."

I turned to George. "George, did you have fun today?"

His tail beat against the duvet. Then he closed his droopy tired eyes and rumbled off to sleep.

In the glow of the bedside lamp with George curled up beside me, I knew we had just had a free day.

I put my book down, turned off the light, put my arm around George and went to sleep.

HERE ARE A FEW LITTLE LESSONS
I LEARNED FROM ONE VERY BIG DOG:

Always swim and surf with a buddy. Both activities are safer and more satisfying that way.

The ocean, like life, can sink you or keep you afloat. Keep your head above the water, and no matter how scary it seems, learn to ride the waves.

Size matters. Whether you're big or small, it's only the size of your heart that counts.

There is no singular way to find love or wisdom. What's important is to recognize when an opportunity for growth presents itself and to accept it with gratitude—whether it comes via an experience, a person . . . or a very big dog.

Epilogue

September 2014

As a little kid, I used to wonder how my grandfather got so smart. How did he know so much about so many different things? As I have gotten older myself, my appreciation for his wisdom has only expanded. Now I often wonder how other older people have acquired their wisdom. I study the hard-earned lines in their faces and can only guess at what experiences brought them to where they are now. Did they become wiser through reading books or through personal successes and failures, or were they just old souls from the time they were born? In the case of George, it's clear his wisdom comes from a combination of his life experience with his innately old soul. I place immense value on his friendship, trust, companionship and, most of all, his love.

After spending two great years together in Hermosa Beach, California, in 2011 George and I returned to Toronto, Ontario, where we now live a quiet—and happy—life. We have found a new community of dogs and their owners in a small park close to where we live downtown. We gather there every morning and every evening, rain or shine. George enjoys his daily play dates with his good pals Molly,

Roxi, Barney, Duffy, Brodie and Howard . . . and any other dog straying into the informal, friendly, furry pack.

We have also added a new family member at home: Charlie the Cat. Charlie was a young, homeless, six-toed cat found wandering the streets when I heard about him through a friend. He is the feline equivalent of George, affectionate and social beyond all standard cat norms. George took to Charlie right away. When Charlie isn't purring on my lap, he's curled against George's warm belly, both of them sound asleep. They are kindred spirits.

I have managed to carve out a new life for myself here in Toronto, one where I look forward to the future and enjoy the present, instead of dwelling on the sadness of the past. I'm pleased to say that I'm in a healthier emotional space now, much happier and even a bit wiser.

George and I made many great friends during our adventure together in L.A. and we took away countless fond memories of our time there. After George's first surfing competition, we continued to surf at Huntington Beach on weekends, and in 2010 George competed in the Surf City Surf Dog championship once again, placing third in the extra-large division and winning the prestigious Crowd Pleaser Award two years running.

This past summer George and I vacationed in Nova Scotia, and spent time at my grandfather's cottage and at Rissers Beach, taking in the waves, the soft white sand and the cold, beautiful ocean. We surfed together again, both of us loving the freedom of being in the waves and riding our board together.

Seeing just how much George loves the sport, I decided to give him one more chance to surf in California. George and I attended the 2014 Surf City Surf Dog competition in Huntington Beach just a few weeks ago.

The same crazy event had grown under Lisa and her team's expert event management. Now there are regularly thousands of

spectators crowding the beach and cheering on the dogs. There are participants from far-flung corners of the world. There are even more cameras and "puparazzi."

George loved being back in California and back at the competition. Many volunteers, competitors and spectators remembered George from years earlier and came out to cheer him on. Despite being tired from a long flight, he held court on the beach, receiving warm hugs and happily posing for pictures with his fans. It was like old times, but with one distinction: George had aged. He was a wiser dog than a few years earlier, but he had also slowed down.

When George's heavyweight heat began, we went charging headlong into the Pacific surf amid cheers from the crowd. The tide was high and the big waves were breaking right on the shore. Many of the dogs, including George, were having a hard time balancing on their surfboards, and after a few failed attempts in the big surf, George swam back to shore and sat down in the sand. After some unsuccessful coaxing, I headed back to the shore to be with my buddy.

When I got there, he looked me in the eye, as he always does. He gave me a few wet kisses and I put my arm around him. "You're tired, big guy. I know. It's okay. Let's just sit here and rest." He gave my face another lick. We sat on the beach and watched as the younger, agile dogs tried their best to get on their boards and surf their way back to shore. George's competitive surfing career had come to an end.

We spent the next few days catching up on sleep and catching up with friends. On the last morning in California, George appeared more energetic and the swagger was back in his step. "Want to go to the beach?" He wagged his tail and looked up at me as only he does, as if to say, "Today I'm totally ready."

I took George off the beaten path that day to the Newport Beach River Jetty, just the two of us. In contrast with the chaos of the surfing

contest a few days earlier, this morning was quiet and peaceful. The sunny beach was deserted except for a few scattered surfers out catching waves. I grabbed our surfboard, clipped on George's leash and we wandered down to the shore.

For the next few hours George rushed into the water alongside me, and he surfed waves like a pro. We ran together in the sand and George chased seagulls. We swam together in the surf, and George let me throw my arms around his neck and towed me back to shore. In between, we lazed on the beach and let the sun warm us.

After a few more blissful hours, it was time to pack up and head to the airport for our trip back to Canada. I put my arms around my big, wet, happy dog. "Time to go home, George," I said. "I love you." He leaned his weight into my chest. I left the leash off as we walked back to the car. He didn't need it anymore. And neither did I.

This is the most important lesson I've learned from George: the path to wisdom is paved with love. All I did to help George was love him. That's all it took. You know the saying "It takes a village to raise a child"? The same is true of anyone in need of rescue, whether neglected animals or human beings—it takes a village to see them through. A lot of people helped George in small and big ways, but for all the love he has received, he has given it back a thousand times over, not only to me but to anyone who ever offered him affection. We should all be as wise as George. It is thanks to him, and in memory of my grandfather, that *free days* from now on will be that much easier to find.

ACKNOWLEDGMENTS

The following people have played a large part in inspiring me and helping bring this book to life. I would like to acknowledge and thank all of them:

To Sandra Nicholson and all of the tremendous volunteers at Newf Friends for all the great work they do in helping Newfoundland dogs in need, and for giving me the opportunity and privilege to adopt George.

To everyone who has had the courage to "save a life" and adopt and love a shelter dog of any breed—these dogs give back every bit of love they get. There is a bit of George in all of these beautiful animals.

Thank you to all the friends I have spent time with at dog parks and beaches over the years—so many great people, dogs and memories. And a big thank you to all my "non-dog" friends for your support and encouragement—in particular, Mike and Cluny Nichols, Matt Kenny, Steve McAllister, Gino Reda, Charlie Horsey, Adam Larry and everyone at MKTG and the NHLPA.

To Catherine and John, Todd and Warren—for your friendship and support in the early years. I miss you very much.

To Cassie and Carole Anne Strong, my "California family," for all the love and support you both gave to George and me, even when

I was lost. It helped and means more to me than you will ever know. Thank you.

To my brother, David—thanks for all of your love, support and encouragement, not just with the book, but with everything we have shared over the years—so proud to have you as my brother.

Thanks to the extraordinary author Lisa Gabriele for planting the seed in my head that I could write this book and for introducing me to Nita (and to Charlie the cat).

Thanks to Evan Rosser for your help in the early days of writing.

Thank you to everyone at Penguin Random House for their hard work and assistance. Thanks to Jennifer Lum for the fabulous book and jacket design. Thanks especially to my amazing editor, Nita Pronovost. Nita, thank you for your friendship, encouragement, mentorship and patience—and for your clear love for George. This would not have happened without you—thank you with all of my heart.

And finally, to George, 140 pounds of fur and love. Your love will always live inside my heart; your fur all over the floor and on my clothes. Both will remain with me forever. You give me so many free days by simply being you—the sweetest, gentlest dog ever.

ORGANIZATIONS TO CHECK OUT

If *Free Days with George* has inspired you to get involved with animal associations in your own community, here are a few suggestions to help you get started. But first, a disclaimer: a Newfoundland dog is a lot of work. They are not for everyone. Adopting George is one of the best things I've ever done, but I am also aware that these dogs require *a lot* of specialized care. Before bringing home any pet, do your research to find an animal that suits your lifestyle and capabilities.

1. Newf Friends: www.newf-friends.ca
This is where I got George, and my first-hand experience is that these volunteers are incredibly caring and helpful. They operate throughout Ontario, Canada, and into some of the neighboring American states. I can't recommend them highly enough!

2. Athletes for Animals: www.athletesforanimals.org
This organization was founded by National Hockey League Players' Association member, David Backes—a great hockey player, animal advocate and captain of the St. Louis Blues. I'm a big fan of David's, both on and off the ice, and I love to support all athletes who help animals in need.

3. Newf Rescue: www.newfrescue.com

Considering rescuing a Newfoundland dog? This website is full of helpful information about the breed, from tips on grooming and training, to an extensive list of Newfoundland rescue clubs across North America.

4. The Humane Society of Canada: www.humanesociety.com

The Humane Society is well known for its work protecting dogs and cats, but did you know they also defend horses and farm animals, lab animals, wildlife and the environment? These folks pound the pavement seven days a week, working across Canada to support animals and other shelters.

5. The American Society for the Prevention of Cruelty to Animals (ASPCA): www.aspca.org

The ASPCA has chapters across the U.S. This organization runs programs that provide local and national leadership in three key areas: caring for pet parents and pets, providing positive outcomes for at-risk animals and serving victims of animal cruelty.

6. The Newfoundland Club of America: www.ncanewfs.org

While this club and its website have a ton of research available online, the NCA is also a parent organization to a large network of regional clubs. If you live in the USA and have a Newfoundland, this is a great resource.

7. The Newfoundland Club UK: www.thenewfoundlandclub.co.uk

If you live in the United Kingdom and are interested in Newfoundland dogs, this club (founded in 1886) has a wealth of information on the breed, its specific health issues, dog shows and more.